One damp dark afternoon as the light began to fade two cloaked figures hailed a taxi. Sitting there watching the London landscape they nervously held the sack of money, half-dreading their mission.

As the taxi pulled up only one of the figures alighted; nervously scuttling across the pavement she urgently rang the bell. A surprised porter read the proffered card and led the masked stranger into the room where a grey haired man sat.

Silently handing over the bag of swag, the intruder backed out as the elderly gentleman began to ask questions. The gang member made a swift get-away into the waiting taxi; all that was left behind was a single note: '**From Ferguson's Gang**'.

FERGUSON'S GANG

The Maidens behind the Masks

Published by Lulu Inc 2013

First published in Great Britain in 2013

www.fergusonsgang.co.uk

ISBN 978-1-291-48453-3

Acknowledgements

A chance sighting of a short article on Ferguson's Gang within the National Trust's Magazine caught my attention. The Gang's story itself was intriguing, enough for me to want to learn more but the added frisson of the anonymity of these young ladies sparked an innate desire to discover who they were.

I had little idea what would be involved when I embarked on this epic journey of discovery. A road that would turn out to span two years and take me all over the UK as I tracked down papers and correspondence that had been hitherto unconnected.

The research into the Gang and the uncovering of their stories has been helped by the cooperation and support of many; in particular I need to thank Vinnie Rorbye for all her professional help on undertaking the research.

The National Trust has been a font of knowledge, allowing access to their archives and papers; my gratitude goes to Darren Beatson for so freely discussing the handed-down knowledge the Trust has of the Gang and Gill Bolton for helping to understand the intricacies of organising donations to the Trust.

The other individuals at Societies who provided help and information include Oliver Hilliam at CPRE, Graham Stevenson on the Communist Party in the 1930s, Penguin Books and the Museum of English Rural Life.

A number of institutions also searched their records for previously undiscovered information; the National Archives, Dr Christopher Hilton and Amelia Walker at the Wellcome Library, the Ecclesiastical Church of Scotland and Janet Doody at the Ironbridge Museum. Linda Moroney at the John Lewis Partnership Archives, Sebastian Wormell at Harrods, Dr Andrea Tanner at Fortnum and Mason and the Red Cross Museum and Archives all provided data which helped piece together the personal stories of the Gang.

Many people who knew the Gang, or were related in some way, kindly gave up their time to share their reminiscences. These include Diana Jervis-Read, Penelope Macgregor, Joanna Bagnall, Polly Bagnall, Virginia Lynch, Philip Pinney and Joyce Conwy-Evans.

Elizabeth Strowlger of the Old Felicians, Mrs Fay of St George's School, Rosemary Moon of North West Kent College and Liz Donlan of St Elphin's Old Girls were also immensely helpful in searching through past records for mentions of the Gang. So too were Channing School's Development Department.

I found all the librarian staff only too willing to take up the challenge of tracking down these maidens, so thanks are extended to Hannah Lowery at Bristol University, Hannah West at Girton College, Anne Thompson at Newnham College, Robert Athol at Cambridge College Archives, Lianne Smith at King's College London Archives, Robert Winckworth and Krisztina Lackoi at UCL, Victoria Rea at the Royal Free London and Ilse Woloszko of the Royal Academy of Music.

In addition thanks go to David Hutchinson at Folkestone Library, Sue Morton and Trish McCormack at Sutton Coldfield Library as well as to the librarians at Essex Library, Steventon Library, Surrey History Centre and Shropshire Archives.

A final word of thanks goes to Richard Ford for allowing unique access to the love letters between Sister Agatha and her lover Harold Jervis-Read. This insight helped to steer the journey of discovery as well as providing an inner vision to the real women behind the masks.

Anna Hutton-North

Contents

Part 1: The Story of Ferguson's Gang

Introduction:

When the National Trust included a short article on Ferguson's Gang in their magazine several years ago, they had little idea of the huge degree of interest it would create. The intrigue around both the Gang's unusual activities and their carefully guarded anonymity sparked a renaissance in their notoriety, starting a race to find out who the Gang were. Previously unrealised correspondence and papers began to be re-examined as clues to the identities were sought.

In these days of instant communications and access to online information it is, perhaps, difficult to imagine how a group of friends were able to pass through society without ever being recognised. It is credit to the Gang members that they did; for almost a hundred years they have retained their cloak of secrecy about them.

The chance discovery of letters between the Gang members though tweaked back this cloak, allowing an enthralling insight into these maidens behind the masks. It prompted a journey of discovery which ran across England and into the lives of eminent politicians, historians and celebrities of the day. The remarkable story of Ferguson's Gang is retold here; it shares not only their outlandish activities, it also reveals the fascinating story behind the Gang.

Never before has the story of Ferguson's Gang been assembled into one place; this makes an attempt to provide a definitive guide for those wanting to find out more and answer the question 'Who were Ferguson's Gang?'.

Chapter One: Who were Ferguson's Gang?

Little was known about this intriguing group of friends who formed in 1927; the Gang's answer was penned by one of the members:

We aint so many, we aint so few:
All of us has this end in view –
National Trust, to work for you.

Green grass turning to bricks and dust,
Stately homes that will soon go bust –
No defence but the National Trust.

Looking at rural England thus
George and Dragon is change for us
Into St. Clough and the Octopus.

Ferguson's Gang has paid its debt,
Ferguson's obligation's met:
Ferguson's Gang has more for you yet.

Information about the Gang is scarce, there are few records to call upon and many of their supporters are no longer alive. It had been established that the Gang was made up of a group of society ladies who were concerned about the wanton destruction of the English countryside. They established themselves in order to fight back and curb the growing urbanisation being witnessed across swathes of English countryside; they took inspiration from other societies such as 'The Apostles', the Cambridge secret sect, and from their schoolroom antics. Each member had their own nom-de-guerre, thus helping preserve their anonymity; continuing with this tradition the members are referred to by these pseudonyms throughout.

The head of the Gang was always proclaimed to be Ferguson; however this figure was elusive and there was some doubt as to whether he actually existed.

The inner-circle of Gang members were: Bill Stickers, Sister Agatha, Lord Beershop of Gladstone Islands and Mercators Projection, Kate O'Brien The Nark and Red Biddy (also known as White Biddy and Shot Biddy). All of these were Edwardian debutantes who came from rich, and often powerful, families; they were well educated, emancipated young ladies who moved amongst the upper echelons of society. In the normal order of things they should have made illustrious marriages, raised families and carried out social engagements; however each rejected this option. The desire to save England may have been their overriding objective but their need to belong strengthened their bond. Each struggled with a difficult home life, beset by troubled relationships with their mothers or the inability to fit into society. The personal stories show the inner battles each gang member fought to find some kind of personal salvation and happiness. This trouncing with tradition formed a uniquely strong bond between the five girls, giving them the opportunity to devote their lives to a more pressing cause; that of saving the England they loved.

A newspaper report of the time described the Gang as being: '...five young Society women in the 'gang'. One is almoner at one of the largest hospitals, and another is 'housekeeper' at a West End hotel. Each is devoted to the preservation of British beauty spots, and they use some of their money to this end.'

For almost a decade the Gang worked unstintingly to actively conserve a heritage that was being lost; as women of the 1930s they held no personal money and yet they were able to raise £4,000 (the equivalent of half a million pounds today) through a network of contacts and acquaintances, conscripting some in as supporters of the Gang and levying others with taxes on their personal wealth. The amount they amassed may, on the face of it, not seem particularly large; however it needs to be remembered that this was against a backdrop of economic crisis –

the Great Depression, mass unemployment and the start of World War II.

The money they raised during this decade supported twelve National Trust appeals and saved five historically important sites and properties; dotted around the country these are permanent reminders of the Gang's contribution.

The Gang were educated well-heeled young ladies who, like their contemporaries, wore Lyle stockings and tweeds and shopped at Harrods and Fortnum and Mason. Yet intriguingly they were worshipers of the natural deities and mystic worlds; enacting rituals of Latin chants as they danced in flowing robes under the moonlit sky; collecting water from the forgotten tributaries of the River Thames and celebrating the four colours of the new dawn.

Keen to live the life of a bandit, the Gang adopted suitable disguises to accompany their pseudonyms, wearing masks while out on assignations; writing in code to arrange meetings and using mockney-English for the report at the end of a mission. They took great delight in charades and games; their payments were always made by a masked representative who presented the money in an unusual format; be it in the carcass of a goose, wrapped around a cigar or even in a miniature liqueur bottle.

A brief account of the Induction of Lord Beershop from the Boo illustrates their love of charades. The Inner Circle of Ferguson's Gang assembled in Sister Agatha's Cell for the ceremony at about 9.25pm with Lord Beershop wearing the Diadem, tunic, cape, liturgical boots and running shorts. Sister Agatha, representing Ferguson by Letters Patient, wore the robes of her order, with wimple, veil and long black gloves. She carried the 'oly oil and the 'oly Ring. Bill Stickers wore jersey, earrings and running shorts. She carried the 'oly 'At. Kate O'Brien T.N. wore official crimson marking robes and carried the 'oly croque. Red Biddy wore a blue satin sacque, scarlet turban and earrings; she carried the liturgical boots while Bill Stickers officiated at the organ. The floral decorations were freesias placed carefully on the altar, illuminated by two red candles. One of the Nine Taoist Genii (He Sicn-Knoo) was present. After the ceremony

4

refreshments were handed round and Is Bludiness danced. The ceremony was finished with a rare print of the liturgical boots.

The Children's Newspaper fully applauded the work of the Gang, in an article accompanied by sketches of the Gang members it declared:

'Ferguson's Gang is active again, but the police have taken no action. Last year, when people were afraid that the 18th-century Shalford Water Mill near Guildford was in danger, a mysterious body of people bought it, had it thoroughly repaired, and presented it to the National Trust, with a 'promised' endowment of £300. In their communications with the National Trust these people signed themselves Ferguson's Gang.

'In January a masked woman walked into the offices of the Trust in Buckingham Palace Gardens, and said she was Red Biddy of Ferguson's Gang. She left a bag containing £100 in silver.

'Months went by. It seemed as if the rest of the promised endowment would not be paid, but the other day a masked man arrived at the offices announcing himself as Erb the Smasher, of Ferguson's Gang. He brought 200 pound notes.

'Is it babyish of these grown-up people to pretend to be mysterious criminals? If so, let us have more babyishness.'

All of this was faithfully recorded in their Boo, together with the minutes of their meetings, records of their assignations and details of the properties they saved; all dedicatedly written or typed up by each member. The first Boo covers the Gang's main period of activity 1927 to 1935 and was handed over to the National Trust during the 1960s. It provides an interesting insight into the meetings held at the Gang's HQ at Shalford Mill. The second Boo, covering the next decade, was recently discovered at a street market and was donated to the National Trust for safe keeping; the records show that the Gang's activities continued on through into the Second World War, something which had not been realised previously.

The Boo (there was no room on the cover for the final 'k') also contained the names of the Gang's supporters and conscripted members. Once again each of these is an elaborate pseudonym so that identification was difficult. The conscripted members included: Granny the Throttler, The Artichoke, Wife of the Artichoke, Poolcat, Erb the Smasher, Fred, Uncle Gregory, Black Maria (or Mary), Silent O'Moyle, Pious Yudhishthira, Joshua Bottle-Washer, Jerry Boham (or Gerry Boham), Sam, Sister Niphite, Is Nib, Outer Yam Yam and Mother Maudez amongst others. The Gang's influence continued to pervade though, finding recruits right up until the end of the twentieth century with Dutch Doll and Pegasus. The Gang's enigmatic charm continues to attract attention even today.

Chapter Two: Lamenting the loss of a beautiful England

Incredible as it may seem now, the destruction and demolition of England's grand country houses was endemic after World War I. The loss of historically important houses during the interwar years' period was becoming a very real issue to the architectural heritage, although not one which was of great public concern. The landed gentry had been demolishing and rebuilding their great houses for the past five hundred years without any consideration for architectural preservation of ancient buildings or consultation with any public body.

From 1900 over 1,000 country houses were demolished in England; in Scotland it was considerably higher. Sometimes these houses were being rebuilt in more modest dimensions allowing for a more economical household with smaller domestic servant requirements but occasionally the sites were simply left fallow.

This wave of demolition reached such a crescendo that it began to raise concern in some quarters of society; the devastation of English country homes was recognised to be irreversible, particularly when architectural gems such as Trentham Hall were demolished with little public interest. Important estates were being destroyed; in fact one in six of all our grand houses were demolished during the twentieth century.

These houses have been collectively termed 'the lost houses'; they included Clumber Park, the principal home of the Dukes of Newcastle. Despite selling a number of other properties and the famous Hope diamond, the family were left with no option but to razor the huge house to the ground in 1938 leaving the Duke without a ducal seat. The Duke of Northumberland was luckier; he was able to sell off Stanwick Park in order to retain Alnwick Castle; and the Duke of Bedford took the decision to considerably reduce Woburn Abbey while selling off other family estates and houses to keep his original ducal seat.

Even the lower-ranked gentility lost their homes; the Godwin-Austen family (the original surveyor of the Himalayas and friend of Bill Stickers) was forced to move out of their family seat at Shalford House, Surrey to live in less imposing quarters.

7

Public outings to watch the demolitions began to become the vogue; Tong Castle, the first example of Gothic architecture in Shropshire, was demolished by the Earl of Bradford on 18 June 1954. One spectator recorded: 'The operation was conducted by the 213 Field Squadron Royal Engineers ...The Church windows were opened to cope with the blast. At 2.30pm. Lord Newport fired the charges ... there are some fine photographs of this event, with the whole base of the Castle covered in smoke'.

Of course some properties were saved by the passionate efforts of a few individuals. When the Duke of Buckingham's stately house at Stowe was under threat of demolition the general attitude was laisse-faire. It is almost unthinkable now but as Merlin Waterson's book *A Noble Thing – the National Trust and its benefactors* noted Country Life was actually in favour of the demolition, citing the house had outlived its usefulness. Clough Williams-Ellis came to the fore; his eloquent praise inspired the Reverend Percy Warrington to consider how these great houses with large open spaces could be re-suited for the modern world as public schools.

Against this backdrop of growing awareness about the loss of country houses was a shift in social thinking towards the benefits of open air and open spaces. The eminent historian GM Trevelyan wrote his book *Must England's Beauty Perish?* which stated: 'Without vision the people perish and without sight of the beauty of nature the spiritual power of the British people will be atrophied.'

Throughout the interwar years there was a general movement that felt as well as protecting the public interests in the open spaces of the country, there should be an opportunity for everyone to have access to these very spaces and not be restricted to the landed gentry. The mass trespass onto the Duke of Devonshire's Derbyshire estate was one such public denunciation against those aristocrats who attempted to prevent walkers, cyclists and swimmers from enjoying the outdoors.

For Ferguson's Gang it was turbulent time; they saw friends and family losing their homes and forced out of their properties. Yet they also agreed with the democratic right of access to beauty for all. The answer, for them, lay in the National Trust.

The Trust had been established in 1884 by the triumvirate of Octavia Hill - a descendent of John Evelyn (the seventeenth century diarist), Canon Rawnsley - the propagandist, and Robert Hunter. The stated aim of the National Trust was to act *as a Corporation for the holding of lands of natural beauty and sites and houses of historical interest to be preserved intact for the nation's use and enjoyment*.

Although it took ten years of hard work to launch the Trust properly, the following forty years saw the National Trust really start to grow in importance; as its subscriber base and list of benefactors grew it began to purchase land and buildings of historical importance in order to ensure permanent preservation for future generations. The first building purchased was Alfriston Clergy House, Sussex, followed by the gifting of Kanturk Castle, Republic of Ireland and Barrington Court, Somerset.

Trevelyan's passionate call in 1929 provided a much needed public boost to the Trust with its moving words: 'Experience and dread necessity have compelled those who care for the preservation of natural beauty to regard the National Trust as their best friend. Every month those who scent the danger in the wind threatening some loved place come to us bearing precious gifts which we are to preserve, not indeed locked away, but as the public heritage... But every increase in the number and area of our properties means increase in our financial liabilities. *We have no central endowment. We have at present less than a thousand annual subscribers. We must get rid of these handicaps if we are to win the race that lies before us.*'

The publication was well timed; it brought the crisis to the public's attention and helped the flagging Trust to re-energise its declining membership and increase subscriptions.

Another well-known advocate of the National Trust was Beatrix Potter, the famous children's author. As well as being an active campaigner during her lifetime she organised for the Trust to be entrusted with almost 4,000 acres in the Lake District, thus preserving an important hill-land way of life, together with almost all the original drawings from her books upon her death.

9

At the National Trust's 1934 Annual Dinner, the Prince of Wales echoed the growing feeling of concern. 'Every town-dweller, every one who can get away for week-ends and very often not even of Saturday afternoons, is clamouring for the preservation – whatever it may be, near London or near our great provisional cities – for the preservation of a retreat.

'The National Trust is really every-one's concerns, and every one can do his part to help it in its great work. We all know, most of us here tonight, the heavy demands that are rightly made on our purses by the many charitable institutions and organisations in this country, but I feel that we have a duty towards our countryside as well. Some people are in the happy position to be able to help by gifts of places of natural beauty or historic interest; others, particularly those who have no immediate heirs, can help by leaving property to the Trust. Failing that, all of us can show our appreciation of what the Trust is doing by simply becoming members and making its important work better known. And if it were better known throughout Great Britain the Trust would be able to do even more than it is doing to-day to preserve those features of British life which have meant so much to those who live in our great cities and indeed to all who love our countryside.'

After much debate the answer was to ensure government protection was obtained to preserve the nationally significant landscapes from haphazard development springing up as a result of a laissez-faire planning system. In response to the Act large tracts of open space were given over to national parks to preserve beauty and allow for recreational access.

This growing backdrop of public interest and access to England's beauty (both landscape and built) together with the social movements occurring provided the tinderbox for the formation of Ferguson's Gang. The publication of Williams-Ellis' *England and the Octopus* proved so influential to them that the Gang felt compelled to take radical action against this destruction of the English countryside and way of life.

Chapter Three: The influence of the Octopus

The interwar period saw England undergo some fundamental shifts in society; the decline of the squirearchy; the move away from large scale domestic servitude; the rise of the working man; and the emancipation of women. The Gang, along with great swathes of the population, were seeing once familiar foundations radically move so that they were in risk of losing traditions overnight and forced into accepting the changes without questioning what was lost.

At the same time the opportunities available to well-educated women were also opening up, the suffrage of women (through the Representation of the People Act of 1918 which gave 8.4m women the vote and enhanced in 1928 when finally all women received the vote on the same terms as men) meant that as well as tertiary education, employment was also now a respectable option for upper-class young ladies. This emancipation benefited the Gang members, allowing them access to a university education which had been denied to their mothers.

The continued fight for suffrage was still on-going though; although the vote had been achieved the next step for many women was to become more politically active. The interwar years saw two of the Mitford sisters (who were not the only aristocratic family involved) to be caught up in Fascist political ideals; Unity Mitford attended the first Nuremberg rally and was a friend to Hitler; her sister, Diana, went on to marry Sir Oswald Mosley. The Communist cause was supported by their sister Jessica Mitford as well as Sylvia Pankhurst and Joan Beauchamp the women suffragettes. It is unsurprising that some of the Gang therefore had strong political inclinations; in fact one member (Red Biddy) even named herself after her Communist beliefs.

As well as the metaphorical landscape undergoing radical changes, so too was the geographical landscape. As the homes of the titled gentry began to fall into disrepair and arrears, their land also became open to those with the right to roam; in addition there was, what some saw as, a worrying spread of housing developments and twee bungalows beginning to spring up as perpetual blots on the landscape.

All of this culminated in the Gang being formed by Bill Stickers in 1927. This fear of the invasion of bungalows was illustrated through one of the Gang's poems:

Up on the cliffs by Mayon Castle,
What 'as you seen to make a fuss?
Upon the cliffs by Mayon Castle
There I seen the Octopus

What was the Octopus a-doing?
East of the Longships as you go?
E'd some bricks and a load o' concrete
For to start on a bungalow…

The Gang members were sensitive to the political tensions around the nation's use and enjoyment of England's countryside which were abound in the early 1930s. There were many who felt that the elements of the aristocracy and landed gentry were now out of touch with the democratic nature of Great Britain. One such believer was Williams-Ellis who wrote: 'One hears and one reads a great deal of sentimental gush about the heart-break of old established landowners forced to sell their ancestral acres through the hardness of times' and blaming it on the owner's 'folly or mismanagement, or… expensive tastes incompatible with the low returns from land owning'.

However Williams-Ellis felt it was unthinkable that these great country houses of England, with their unique architecture, associations and beauty of setting should be lost. He rallied the cause, taken up subsequently by Country Life, to identify the most significant country houses in order that these were somehow preserved for posterity. He also went on to write 'his angry little book' entitled *England and the Octopus* in 1927 about the urbanisation of the countryside.

Williams-Ellis provided to be an exemplar for the Gang; before writing his book Williams-Ellis had been heavily involved with the Council for the Protection of Rural England (CPRE), the

National Trust (through his friendship with GM Trevelyan) and the society set up by William Morris, of the Arts and Crafts movement, to protect ancient buildings (SPAB).

He was devoted to retaining regional styles and his keen interest in preserving buildings spawned from a distinctive architectural career that spanned half a century; he ironically accredited his success to luck and three months technical training at the Architectural Association against Lutyens' mere three weeks. Portmeirion, the Italianate village in North Wales is his best known work and legacy.

Married to Amabel, a member of the Baronet Strachey of Sutton Court family, he wore his clothes with panache; cutting a sight with his cravat or bow-tie, bright coloured waistcoats and long jackets invariably worn with breeches and long knitted yellow stockings, and at least one member of Ferguson's Gang claimed to be in love with this 'bird of paradise'.

Both Merlin Waterstone and Claire Riche mention the touching inscription in one of the Gang member's copy of *England and the Octopus*; Williams-Ellis wrote 'to whom I would have Dedicated this Angry Little Book, had she been known to me when I wrote it.' He was a natural storyteller and raconteur and it is no surprise that he was able to spark such an interest in the decline of England's country houses.

The octopus mentioned within the title of his book is a reference to Lord Curzon's speech of 1913. Lord Curzon formally opened Colley Hill, Surrey for the National Trust and bestowing the virtues of the Trust's work in saving the property for posterity called London 'a great octopus stretching its tentacles in order to lay hold of the rich pastures and leafy lanes of the countryside'.

Williams-Ellis's resulting words provoked great reaction: 'This has largely destroyed the remaining amenity of the town, and has raised the rates by reason of the expensive drainage and other public services entailed by this malformation of the town by 'tentacle growth'.'

The publication of his book coincided with developers' plans to buy and build on Stonehenge; this debate caught national attention and the National Trust launched a public appeal in 1927

13

to purchase the 2,100 acres of Stonehenge Down (including the Neolithic monument of Stonehenge) to prevent development on the fields around the monument.

Williams-Ellis espoused the need to protect the area from any further invasion; 'As it now is, Stonehenge is intolerable, and by no means to be visited save by blind archaeologists. Hemmed in by iron railings, guarded by a turn-stile and a post-card kiosk, glowered at by the derelict aerodrome and smirked at by café and bungalow, this sacred place is indeed painful beyond bearing.'

This call to arms by Williams-Ellis was a passionate re-invigoration of Ruskin's *Fors Clavigera*. 'The sun had drawn landscapes for you... in green and blue and all imaginable colours, here in England. Not one of you ever looked at them then; not one of you cares for the loss of them now, when you have shut the sun out with smoke. There was a rocky valley between Buxton and Bakewell, once upon a time, divine as a vale of Tempe...The valley is gone, the gods with it.'

This zealous appeal and the fear of losing such a sacred site of worship galvanised Bill Stickers. She brought together a band of friends and created Ferguson's Gang. The passionate war cry forced them into taking direct action against the growing urbanisation. They actively supported saving large tracts of land, gaining recognition for their efforts. Their greatest difference though was their determination to actually bring the essence of Williams-Ellis' book to life. They personified his views of: 'the chief obligations would be to maintain the fabric of the house and such part of its surrounding demesne as might be scheduled with it in an adequate and conservative fashion; to submit to authority on all questions of major alterations; and to grant the public certain statutory privileges of access under carefully framed conditions.'

Like no other group before them, the Gang radically changed the way the National Trust operated; they not only identified historically important properties but also undertook to repair and renovate the buildings. They made sure that time honoured techniques were used so that the sympathetic restoration would allow the buildings to continue to be used throughout the next century. This thinking was far ahead of their time; it may be

14

common place now but at that time most buildings were merely being sold off for scrap.

The Gang retained their lifelong dedication to the cause; they were interested in saving what they saw as the very core of Englishness. As Williams-Ellis said: 'What would the country be without its buildings? The English countryside is landscape in harness, and the most substantial consisted of 'simple, vernacular villages… which grew bit by bit, round the church and along the main street', taking in the 'squire's house, the vicarage and one or two other buildings.' It was this part of England's heritage that the Gang fought so hard to save.

Chapter Four: Establishing a Constitution

The close knit Gang members stayed together through every adversity over the next decade; the Gang formed a family unit for them, filling the gap left by their unhappy home lives. Each girl suffered from a troubled parental relationship, was frequently unwell and found it difficult to adjust to society's expectations for young debutantes of that time. The Gang provided them with an outlet for their liberated views on women's emancipation; the other girls provided an emotional support and uncensored caring environment that allowed each one to be themselves.

The Gang was formed with the intention of halting urbanisation through philanthropic means; they recognised that if they wanted to save properties then they were going to need money. Over the course of a decade the Gang successfully amassed over half a million pounds (in today's money) which they used to save seventeen properties and sites. With no access to personal money, although each member was of a wealthy family, they were forced to be inventive. They collected, sought out and raided friends for any Victorian coinage – the value of silver being high at the time. They also conscripted members to join, forcing them to pay a high subscription in return for a Gang pseudonym and chance to join in the fun; they also levied taxes on family wherever possible, seeking out aunts, parents and grandparents to support them. Most of the money came in this way; however the outlandish activities of some members procured finances in a totally different fashion. Kate O'Brien accosted visiting residents at the most exclusive London hotels where she worked in order to support the cause while Red Biddy took a far more direct approach. After a raucous dinner at the Dorchester she stole the entire stock of toothpicks and ransomed them back to raise funds. The end justified the means; they approached the need for obtaining money with the same joie-de-vivre that they approached life.

The Gang continued to meet up after leaving university; attending Bill Sticker's wedding, visiting Sister Agatha's flat and visiting Red Biddy's family home at Racedown but the first official meeting of Ferguson's Gang was not until five years later. On 26th March 1932 Ferguson, Sister Agatha, The Lord Beershop, Bill Stickers, Kate O'Brien T.N. and Red Biddy officially founded Ferguson's Gang.

This meeting set out the Gang's serious intentions to take action against the developers and demolition men. A number of items were discussed and recorded in the Boo but two fundamental propositions were agreed. Firstly that the number of the inner-circle of Gang members should be limited to five due to the 'difficulty raised of accommodating eight on drum over grindstone which comfortably seats five'; this grindstone was in the mill which would eventually become their official HQ. They also decided that the number of supporters and members would not be limited, thus ensuring adequate funds could be raised to support the Gang's activities. The result of this decision meant a number of family members and close friends were actively petitioned and enrolled who went on to become conscripted members.

The second proposal was to draw up a constitution that gave a very clear remit for their activities. Whatever anyone else thought of the Gang they remained united and single-mindedly focused. Their constitution outlining the rules of the club was drawn up at this first meeting and each member signed in what looks like blood.

The constitution was occasionally updated and added to; mainly it would appear at the suggestion of the Gang member known as Lord Beershop. When the Gang visited Stonehenge to view it after the National Trust's public appeal had successfully saved it in 1927 a new ritual was created for celebrating the 'saving of Stonehenge'.

The Constitution:

1. Ferguson's Gang shall be known as FERGUSON'S GANG.
2. The object of the Gang shall be to follow the precepts of Ferguson in destroying and frustrating the OCTOPUS.
3. The Gang shall consist of no more Active Members than can be accommodated upon the drum of the grindstone on the west side, their feet being inside the said drum; and of an unlimited number of subscribing members.
4. It shall be permissible for an absent Active Member to provide a deputy at meetings.
5. Active Members shall be required to produce at the meeting all the Victorian coinage they have been able to save during the preceding period.
6. Subscribing members shall be such as on payment of a subscription are authorised to take a name in the Gang.
7. Election of new Active Members shall be by inspection, followed by secret ballot.
8. The member on being elected shall place one hand on the shaft of the mill and publicly pronounce these words: '*I swear to follow Ferguson in preserving England and frustrating the Octopus.*'

It was at this meeting that the Gang conspired to become a shadowy anonymous group; modern-day Robin Hoods whose elaborate charades and outlandish pseudonyms helped to fuel this dashing cavalier image. This on the whole was accepted; the newspapers and press played up the masked bandit theme, helping the Gang to further their cause even more.

There were some though within the general public who misunderstood the Gang's explicit philanthropy; the National Trust's Bulletin carried an intriguing paragraph. 'The attention drawn to 'Ferguson's Gang' in the Press must be held responsible for the inmate of a mental home writing to ask 'Ferguson's Secret Philanthropic Society' to supply him at once with 10 guineas wherewith to buy books and instruments for the study of 'Chaldean astrol (sic) Science.' There is no record of whether the Gang ever responded to this request.

Yet there was a serious side to the Gang; they determined to actively save as much English countryside as they possibly could. With so many stately homes being destroyed they realised their attempts to stop the general tide would be futile. Instead they looked at the ways they could support an existing established organisation.

The two obvious ones were the CPRE and the National Trust. In the end the Gang agreed that it would be more appropriate to support the National Trust; the Trust's aim of 'holding of lands of natural beauty and sites and houses of historical interest to be preserved intact for the nation's use and enjoyment' embodied their own beliefs. The Gang may also have been influenced by personal friendships with Williams-Ellis, GM Trevelyan and the British Prime Minister all of whom were existing high-profile National Trust supporters.

While the girls knew there were limits to the funds they could access, Bill Stickers was obviously an inspiring leader of their cause; when one of the Gang members attended the 1934 National Trust AGM, she reported back that the incoming Secretary wanted to save both large and small houses, and added in typical Gang-mockney: 'I think umbly Sire that Bill ad better not be toald this or e may go orf the deep end & come and dere Winsor Carsol or Catsworf or Nole as the Gangs contribushun to the skeme'! As it was the Gang sensibly concentrated their efforts on preserving quintessential village architecture.

The use of their codes, disguises and pseudonyms was to preserve their anonymity; they were desperate to keep away from public detection. There must have been a frisson of concern about whether the Gang's anonymity would be exposed when a question over publicising donors to the National Trust was raised by an MP during questions to the Prime Minister at the House of Commons in 1933. Hansard records Mr Hall-Caine asking whether the Prime Minister would consider the desirability of devising some form of public recognition for those persons who presented to the National Trust, for permanent preservation by the nation, places of natural scenic beauty.

The response of the Prime Minister, Ramsay MacDonald, was evasive no doubt briefed by Baldwin, perhaps at the behest of the Gang. He said 'I am sure that everyone will applaud, as I do, the public spirit of those who preserve places of natural beauty for the perpetual enjoyment of the public. I doubt whether it would be wise or graceful to try and stereotype any form of public approbation, but if my hon. Friend has any suggestions to make I will certainly consider them.' The decision to continue to allow donations to remain anonymous must have pleased the Gang.

Chapter Five: The Gang from 1927 to 1939

The first Boo records that the Gang officially met thirteen times from 1927 to 1935, however they kept in close contact at all times, going on holiday together and meeting up for dinner. The Gang formed a second, more permanent, family unit for the girls which meant they often turned to one another for support during this time.

1927

The friendship between Bill, Agatha and Kate blossomed in their year at college; away from their studies they began to enact the same kind of antics that Bill had persuaded her friends to undertake at Cambridge. This time though Bill wanted to form something more enduring and the publication of *England and the Octopus* gave a purposeful direction; the creation of Ferguson's Gang was therefore perfect. When the Gang was first created there was an additional King's College member (See Mee Run). They cemented the friendship with their official banquet.

Official Banquet - 27th May
Present: Ferguson, Bill Stickers, Sister Agatha, Kate O'Brien and See Mee Run.

Taking inspiration from the Cambridge Apostles through Erb the Smasher's tales, Bill Stickers formed Ferguson's Gang. The banquet was held while all four of the girls were still attending King's College; as the summer term ended so Bill Stickers left to become married.

Having formed the Gang they set about saving small coinage wherever possible to make donations but what Bill really wanted was a huge project that the Gang could really make a difference with. An idea of how this could be carried out began to germinate when a close neighbour of Bill Stickers, the second Lord Tennyson, presented a large plot of land on the Isle of Wight to the National Trust in memory of his father. This donation sparked a realisation of what the Gang could accomplish by

21

supporting the Trust and they began considering their fund raising in earnest.

1928

Bill Stickers married Old Uncle Gregory at the family church, St Margaret's, Westminster on 1st July 1928 with little of the usual pomp and circumstance which surrounded a high society wedding. They set up home in London initially. In contrast Sister Agatha's relationship with Harold Jervis-Read continued, becoming more complex and confusing for her as she tried to deal with the consequences of having a married lover.

Later that summer Sister Agatha and Bill Stickers travelled down to Cornwall for a holiday to enjoy a restful sojourn at St Ives; for both it was painful time. Sister Agatha had failed her degree examinations and needed to consider her future plans while Bill realised that her marriage with Uncle Gregory would continue to go unconsummated. The holiday allowed both girls a break from their worries.

Upon their return Sister Agatha decided to leave King's College and began training as an Almoner; she moved out of the hostel and into lodgings where she met fellow lodger Lord Beershop.

1929

The Gang began to leave King's College; Kate O'Brien graduated and began working at an illustrious London hotel and Sister Agatha attended the London School of Economics as part of her Almoner training. They were all still living in London when they agreed to initiate Lord Beershop into the Gang.

The publication of Professor Trevelyan's passionate appeal *Must England's Beauty Perish?* prompted the Gang to begin selecting National Trust appeals to support; the first one was chosen because of Lord Beershop's and Kate O'Brien's family homes' being close to Cheshire. They collected money from friends, raising £1 for the Chester appeal.

Chester Roman Amphitheatre - £1 donation

The discovery of the amphitheatre in 1929 unearthed the reputedly largest Roman amphitheatre in Britain, dating from the 1st century. It was built by the Legio II *Adiutrix* and had fallen into disuse around 350 A.D. It fascinated the Gang with its historical significance.

1930

The Gang expanded, on Sister Agatha's suggestion they welcomed Red Biddy as an inner-circle member, making the Gang a total of six girls. They weren't together for long though, the girls were beginning to drift away from London. Bill Stickers and Uncle Gregory moved out of London down to Cornwall, Lord Beershop completed her studies and Sister Agatha found a placement working in Norwich, making it more difficult for the Gang to meet up regularly.

1931

This was a quiet year for the Gang; it saw the eventual inner-circle members being finalised with See Mee Run being executed by the Gang as a traitor and a nark. In reality she probably married and moved away; no further reference was ever made to her existence.

For Red Biddy the elation at having passed her first year exams was followed by disappointment when she failed her finals at Bristol causing her to look elsewhere for her medical degree. She decided to join King's College and enrolled there for the October term.

Lord Beershop, having completed her studies, went on a Caribbean cruise before returning home to work as a freelance artist; Sister Agatha took up a training position at The General Infirmary, Leeds and Kate O'Brien began to work for another hotel owned by Gordon Hotels.

The impositions of work meant the Gang were confined on when they were able to meet up. They continued to raise money to support the Trust's appeals, raising £5 for Hindhead, a site close to Bill Stickers' childhood home.

Hindhead Appeal - £5 donation
The site at Hindhead, South Downs, West Sussex was 37 acres purchased on 3rd March 1931 from Louisa Charlotte Tynall.

1932

1932 marked a watershed year for Ferguson's Gang. They went from occasional small donations to becoming a fully-fledged group of bandits who were intent on making a difference. The ideal opportunity to make the difference arose when Bill and Sister Agatha travelled down to Cranleigh to celebrate Pious Yudhishthira's marriage. Passing through the countryside they spied an old water mill. The building potentially provided the answer to their two problems; concern at the difficulty in easily meeting up beset the Gang (it was becoming increasingly obvious that the Gang needed their own headquarters) and how to show they were serious about saving England's heritage.

By saving Shalford Mill, Guildford they solved both in one go. The design of the water mill meant the property was naturally split into a habitable living area and the working area which housed the grind stone, wheels and mechanics, thus providing them with their quirky headquarters.

The Old Mill at Shalford, Surrey – purchased and restored by the Gang for £500
Bill and Sister Agatha sought out the owners of the mill and discovered that it was part of Pious Yudhishthira's beleaguered estate. They arranged to buy the attractive four-storey timber framed brick and hung-tile eighteenth-century watermill. The money required to purchase the mill came mainly from parents; the Gang had not set up a network of subscribing members at this point who they could levy.

The mill was in a bad state having fallen into disrepair after the First World War. It had last been used as a working corn mill in 1914 but the building had miraculously remained almost unaltered.

The view of the bridge over the stream was reputed to have been the inspiration for local artist, Ernest Shepard, only a few years before as the setting for his famous illustration of AA Milne's character Christopher Robin peering down into the water while playing 'Pooh Sticks' (not to be confused with Ashdown Forest which was Milne's inspiration for the story).

Purchasing the mill gave Ferguson's Gang the potential headquarters they needed. Immediately they wrote to the National Trust on pale blue paper requesting the Trust rent the room to them: 'Ferguson's Gang salutes the National Trust asks if the Gang may rent from the Trust a small room in the attic in the main body of the Mill, overlooking the Mill Head, very difficult of access by visiting public and of no particular interest except to Ferguson's Gang.

'Ferguson's Gang offers the National Trust a rent of £3 p.a. for the use of this room.

'Ferguson's Gang also hopes, all being well, to complete the endowment of the Mill this year.

'And your petitioners will ever pray.'

Their meetings usually took place at the weekend, arranged so they could meet when Kate O'Brien and Sister Agatha were not working and Red Biddy was not studying. The meetings, carefully recorded in The Boo, plotted the changing lives of the girls over this time; Sister Agatha was absent for a number of meetings when she was working abroad and Red Biddy changed her name to White Biddy and then Shot Biddy. The reports by each of the Gang members after their assignations were also held within the Boo.

The frequent mentions of Ferguson are intriguing; it may well be that it was part of the on-going subterfuge to maintain the illusion that Ferguson was actually involved; there is no evidence to suggest that Ferguson ever attended in person except for the records in the Boo.

Each girl would travel to Shalford Mill, weighed down with their Victorian coinage excitedly looking forward to the meeting and the lavish dinners which would be delivered by Fortnum and Mason. The records are a curious combination of flippancy and seriousness; they were intent on having fun but nothing stood in their way of continuing to 'destroy the octopus'.

First meeting – 26th March 1932
First meeting – 26th March 1932
Those present: Ferguson, Sister Agatha, Lord Beershop, Bill Stickers, Kate O'Brien and Red Biddy

The meeting immediately starts with a recollection that a mosquito was annoying the members, apparently under the orders of Lord Beershop who was called upon to exert proper control over it. They moved on to the more serious discussions of further acquisitions although details of these potential properties aren't recorded.

As mentioned previously they discussed the size of the grind stone determining how large the inner-circle of the Gang should be – could more be squeezed in? Red Biddy though managed to persuade the others to keep the existing numbers by pointing out that remaining at the current size meant the Gang could travel cheaper by car at 25/2d a day.

It was at this meeting that the Gang drew up and signed their constitution as well as passing a number of resolutions. The first was 'That ENGLAND is STONEHENGE, and not WHITEHALL.' The second resolution was 'LUNCH'.

They feasted on lobster cutlets, potato salad, raspberry cream, fresh pineapple and Old Malinsey (Malmsey wine) before heralding a series of toasts to: England, the National Trust, Pious Yudhishthira - donor of the mill, their next meeting and finally Ferguson and his Gang.

The minutes were signed off with the phrase 'Sanginarius Merc & Glad'. The phrase is a fictitious statement conjured up by Lord Beershop's imagination and is a play on a 'religious' blessing.

May 10th 1932

A signed receipt from the National Trust shows that the Gang made their first 'official' donation having once again raided the pockets of their friends for the money.

Second meeting – 5th June 1932
Kate O'Brien was absent from the meeting

The Gang discussed their latest two donations to the National Trust; the Watersmeet appeal and the Golden Valley appeal. They had collected £1 8s 3½d in Victorian silver and discussed suitable dates for their proposed trip to Stonehenge (which was sent in code by letter to Kate). Halfway through the meeting Ferguson looked in, wearing a remarkable disguise. The meeting ended with lunch.

Watersmeet Preservation Scheme - £5 donation

Kate's love of Devon promoted the Gang to support the Watersmeet, Lynmouth, Devon appeal; it was not far from Woolacombe where she would go to stay. The 2,000 acres that were saved included Britain's deepest river gorge, the valleys of the East Lyn and Hoar Oak Water and the woodlands of Lyn Valley.

Golden Valley Preservation Scheme – 14s donation

In contrast the support for Golden Valley was promoted by Red Biddy's acquaintance with Marie Stopes, the pioneer in birth control. The Trust acquired 97 acres from Marie Carmichael Stopes and a further 10 acres from Sarah Lawrence.

Third meeting – 16th October 1932
Lord Beershop, Sister Agatha, Bill Stickers, Kate O'Brien and Red Biddy

This was the auspicious outing to Stonehenge which they had discussed at the last meeting; having assembled at Waterloo to catch the 11am train to Salisbury they arrived at 1.05pm and were collected by their waiting chauffeur who drove them along the course of the River Avon to Stonehenge. As they watched the passing landscape they were delighted to find it was totally unspoilt; the nearest buildings were unobtrusive and with a clear skyline on nearly all sides. After arriving they decanted to the monolithic site and carried out the planned ritual and noted with a degree of satisfaction that there were no other people present to view this ceremony.

The ceremony (from the Boo):

1. On entering the precincts Is Bludiness will utter the words ALE STONEHENGE. And all the Gang shall reply ALE STONEHENGE.

2. Is Bludiness shall then place Imself at the head of a procession, followed immediately by Ferguson, and then in couples by Bill Stickers and Sister Agatha, and Kate O'Brien The Nark and Red Biddy. E shall take the most convenient route, to be decided upon as a result of inspection upon the spot, to the stone known 2 the Public as the Slaughter Stone.

3. On reaching the Slaughter Stone E shall take up a commanding position and turning 2 the Gang shall bless them with the words ALE GANG. To which the Gang shall reply ALE BEERSHOP.

4. Is Bludiness shall then receive from Sister Agatha the pen of dedic8ed sheep, while the Gang addresses Im with these words: MAY IT PLEASE YOUR BLUDINESS 2 SACRIFICE THESE DEDIC8ED SHEEP. And Is Bludiness shall ceremonially enquire WOT 4. And the Gang shall equally ceremonially in4m Im: 4 THE PRESERVATION OF ENGLAND & THE DESTRUCTION OF THE OCTOPUS. And Is Bludiness shall further ceremonially enquire: WHEN YEW SAY ENGLAND DO YOU MEAN ENGLAND

AS REPRESENTED BY WHITEHALL OR ENGLAND
AS REPRESENTED BY STONEHENGE. And all the
Gang shall reply ceremonially STONEHENGE.

5.   The Beershop being thus satisfied that E is doing the Right Thing shall deposit the dedic8ed sheep on the Slaughter Stone, returning the pen and other matters 2 Is pocket lest the Bye Laws concerning Litter be offended. And all the Gang shall say ALE ENGLAND.

6.   Is Bludiness shall then be presented with a Souvenir and an Illumin8ing Address, to which E shall ceremonially reply THANK YEW ALL.

7.   The Gang shall then ceremonially lay their hands upon the appropriate upright stone and observe one minute's silence by a second and watch held by the Beershop.

8.   The Beershop shall cause the one minute's silence 2 be termin8ed with the words STOP.

9.   The Gang shall go home.

After they finished touring the site the Gang caught the 5.55pm back to London, although the return journey was not without incident. At Porton, just outside Salisbury, Bill was rescued in desperate extremity by Ferguson, who then lost his nerve and bolted at Andover.

The rest of the journey was taken up with discussions around finances and of their own personal battles to 'fight the octopus'. Lord Beershop updated everyone on the outrage of the octopus in Wales (this may be to do with the area near to Joshua Bottle-Washer's house where Beershop would go and stay); Kate on her successful dealing with the litter nuisance at Woolacombe and Bill's successful fight for a footpath.

The journey ended with two resolutions; firstly 'That this has been a lovely day' and secondly 'That the Gang may now go to sleep'.

Fourth meeting – 10th December 1932
All members were present except Kate O'Brien

They started out sitting on the grind stone and discussed the three Acts (or Ags as they are referred to) which were, again, faithfully recorded in the Boo. Having agreed them the Gang moved into the neighbouring room for the sake of warmth!

Lord Beershop described the victory over the octopus in Wales (but frustratingly without any mention of what the battle was over) before Bill gave an update on further successes in Cornwall. This was succeeded by Lord Beershop suggesting the 'incorporation of Is Advisers' in the outer circle of Ferguson's Gang, and promulgated an invitation from their Lordships for the Gang to stay with them when visiting Chester. This visit was provisionally fixed for the second weekend before Easter.

'Their Lordships' presumably refers to Lord Beershop's parents who lived in the Midlands; and the reference to Chester is in relation to their donation for the appeal to save the Roman amphitheatre at Chester.

The meeting went on to talk about the first instalment of £100, which was due to the National Trust as the initial payment for Shalford Mill, and how the drop should be made. Red Biddy and Kate O'Brien were nominated to convert the money in to half-crowns and to make the delivery fully-masked.

The National Trust Dinner was coming up and the Gang decided to go wearing black velvet and masks, keeping their personalities hidden. The meeting ended with Lord Beershop presenting medals and titles to the Group and electing Kate to be the 'Bearer of the Travelling Bag'. The resolution was passed 'That the Gang shall now go out for a run'.

At this fourth meeting the Gang began to revel in theatrical antics with three new acts, duly introduced by Bill Stickers, Lord Beershop and Sister Agatha, and required outlandish pomp and circumstance to accompany them.

First Act – Bill Stickers His Act 1932

The first was headed up '*Bill Stickers His Act, 1932*' and illuminated with a W in the top left hand corner and a seal on the right:

FERGUSONS GANG
Do hereby confer, vest and endow IS BLUDINESS THE LORD BEERSHOP OF THE GLADSTONE ISLANDS AND MERCATORS PROJECTION upon, in and with ABSOLUTE AUTHORITY AND POWER to decide questions of POLICY, disputes of a PERSONAL NATURE, GRIEVANCES, alternative PLANS OF ACTION, whether FINANCIAL, PROPAGANDIST, NEGOTIATORY, LOCAL, REGIONAL, NATIONAL or MISCELLANEOUS.

CLAUSE A.
It shall be deemed a dangerous and reprobale HERESY, SIGN of DISAFFECTION, BACKSLIDING and OCTOPOPHILLY for any member of the Gang to profess, imply or otherwise give vent to any opinion that IS BLUDINESS THE LORD BEERSHOP IS IN THE WRONG:
ALWAYS PROVIDED
That a member of the Gang labouring under a GENUINE SENSE OF INEQUITABLE PROCEDURE may in a modest and non-provocative manner observe, that in the opinion of such a Member IS BLUDINESS HAS BEEN MISADVISED BY IS ADVISERS.
CLAUSE B.
Matters of such importance that they are UNABLE to stand over till a GENERAL MEETING of the Gang may be communicated to IS BLUDINESS in writing; but small and local questions may be decided, in a case of GREAT URGENCY and the UNAVOIDABLE ABSENCE of IS BLUDINESS, by IS BLUDINESSES ACONITE.
SUBSECTION i.
In cases of the aforementioned of the whole matter together with the ruling of IS BLUDINESS shall be FULLY PROMULGATED at the next General Meeting of the Gang.
CLAUSE C.
It shall be the UNCHANGEABLE POLICY of Ferguson's Gang to maintain, even in the FACE OF DIRECTLY CONTRADITORY EVIDENCE, that THE CHURCH CAN DO NO WRONG: and this reply shall be deemed a SUFFICIENT and SUITABLE answer to all enquiries.
To which provisions witness this tenth day of December 1932 our hands and Seal of Ferguson's Gang.

This was signed by Sister Agatha A.B., Bill Stickers, pp Kate O'Brien T.N. and Red Biddy.

Second Act – Finance Ag

The second one was headed up FINANCE AG of Is Bludiness the Lord Beershop of the Gladstone Islands & Mercators Projection, Dec 10 1932 and has the footprint of a Boa Constrictor at the end.

CLAUSE A.
WHEREAS WE SANGUINARIUS by the dispensation of Providence BEERSHOP of the Gladstone Islands and Mercators Projection, have been PLEASED to institute and promulgate the following AG or BILL dealing with the FINANCES of FERGUSONS GANG:
CLAUSE B.
By the Provisions of BILL STICKERS' AG of Dec 10 1932 IT SHALL BE DEEMED A DANGEROUS AND REPROBABLE HERESY, SIGN OF DISAFFECTION, BACKSLIDING AND OCTOPOPHILLY FOR ANY MEMBER OF THE GANG TO PROFESS......THAT IS BLUDINESS THE LORD BEERSHOP IS IN THE WRONG:
CLAUSE C.
THEREFORE We do promulgate this Ag or Bill in the full Consciousness that NO MEMBER OF FERGUSONS GANG will challenge or dispute Our Authority; and that Our Promulgation will be taken as a sufficient Endorsement of the VALIDITY thereof.
CLAUSE D.
WHEREAS it seems to Us that the finances of Ferguson's Gang do prosper, and that the diversion of a modicum of the same is in Our opinion innocent, justifiable and reasonable:
CLAUSE E.
We do therefore institute the principle of a TRAVELLING BAG, to be maintained and kept by such person as We in Our Discretion shall appoint:
CLAUSE F.
And into such Travelling Bag shall be put contributions towards the Costs of Journeys made by Ferguson's Gang in the Service of England and the Frustration of the Octopus.
CLAUSE G.
And it shall be Our Principle at meetings of the Gang to call upon said Custodian of the Travelling Bag for statements, as in Our Discretion shall seem best.
CLAUSE H.
And in this, as in other matters, Our Judgement, Interpretation, Elaboration or Manipulation of the Clauses of this Ag or Bill shall be EXETER CATHEDRAL and not open to Question. To which We set Our PERSONAL SEAL of a Boa Constrictor's Footprint.......

Third Act – Ag's Seal Act, 1932

The third act is Ag's Seal Act, 1932 and has the four signatures of the Gang, with Red Biddy in her characteristic red ink, and finished off with a wax seal. It appears that Kate O'Brien T.N. was absent as Bill Stickers wrote pp Kate O'Brien; this probably accounts for why there is no act by Kate at this meeting.

WE FERGUSON'S GANG DO HEREBEY ENACT DECLARE and AFFIRM that all Documents issued by us shall be ratified by ONE of our SEALS: TO WIT:-

THE GREAT SEAL, to be employed by Ferguson's Gang acting in concert with the LORD BEERSHOP.

The SECULAR SEAL, to be employed by Ferguson's Gang ONLY in ADDRESSES or PETITIONS to the LORD BEERSHOP or IS ADVISERS.

THE LORD BEERSHOP'S PRIVY SEAL of a Boa Constrictor's footprint, to be employed by the LORD BEERSHOP acting independently, or in CASE OF EMERGENCY with the authority of the GREAT SEAL.

To which provisions witness this tenth day of December 1932, our hands and the Seal of Ferguson's Gang.

1932 proved to be a rich year for the Gang; as well as making a number of donations to large appeals across England they secured the future of the Old Mill at Shalford and in doing so found their headquarters.

It was less fortunate for Sister Agatha personally though; she had seen Jervis-Read finally move out from his marital home with Marjory to set up the life of a single man away from his family. Frustratingly though he was still inaccessible to her as a potential husband. In addition Agatha witnessed her own parents' marriage breakdown; the emotional turmoil within the family became so unbearable that her parents legally separated.

1933

The start of the year brought the concern of providing the first instalment of money for the Old Mill. Kate O'Brien and Red Biddy were charged with writing up detailed reports of their mission.

22nd January 1933 – report of Kate O'Brien The Nark, G.D. Deposit for Shalford Mill

To Bill Stickers.

On receipt of check I hid same in secret drawer & phoned Red Biddy. A meeting was arranged for the next afternoon at 2.30 outside the bank. I started early in case I had to dodge the tecks. On arrival I found Biddy already there with a lamp having chained her cycle to back of Bank. We went in & presented check. We were asked to wait 10 mins while they opened a strong room for the swag. The money was given us in a neat sack. Very heavy. We procured Taxi. Loaded the swag & proceeded towards Victoria unfollowed. In taxi we removed Biddy's topcoat and fixed mask. Document was unwrapped but left in undervest. Card was produced and all madd ready for presentation. On arrival it was almost dusk. The Trust had a lighted bow window onto street. I hoped they would receive Red Biddy there, then I could have observed whole interview. Biddy scuttled across pavement with card, document & sack. Porter let her in & took card into lighted office. General commotion followed. Card was inspected by all & then taxi examined through window. I lay back on seat to avoid detection. Taxi man looked worried & stopped engine. I got ready to shoot. Greyhaired man got up and went out to interview Biddy. Report of interview will be given by her. She was later shown out by grey-haired man. Others watching from window. We took taxi back to Victoria to cover our tracks dived underground & scattered.

26th January 1933 – Report of Red Biddy, G.D.

On that momentous day Kat & I as a date outside Barclay's Bank at 2.30 – Well believe it or not Bill I gets there at 2.10 and have stabled my horse and am looking round for somewhere to hide from the police till Kate should come....When Kate turned up – well we said – This is luck, & in we goes to the bank ever so brave like. & up walks Kate to the man behind the cage & says I wants a undred pounds – Well the man tried on a bit of bluff & says "Do I know you?" an all that game, but Kate

34

give him her private password & he says orl right but you must wait. So Kate & I goes & sits down on the bench &…wen we was fed up with waiting…up walks Kate to the man behind the cage, & there was the undred pounds all the time ready & waiting - …I carry the bag & Kate gets a taxi & off we go to the Trust. I puts on my mask & the Taxi man wasn't suspicious so all went well & we gets to the Trust – Well Kate sits in the taxi & I goes up to the door & says to the man at the door – Ear's my card – please give it to the Secretary of the National Trust – Well e looks at me suspicious like & sez av yer got an appointment? I sez 'no, but the Secretary will see me when e sees my card' – Well off he gose hesitating like & back he comes, & the Secretary, a dear old man, sez 'Come this way please'. So im & I goes into a Private room like & he sez 'sit down please, we are always very pleased to see the gang.' He was such a nice gent & he was dressed in city gents black & he was so nice & gentle loike that I quite took to im. Well I sez 'Oi av been instructed by Fergersens Gang to present to you the sum of one hundred pounds & an illuminated address.' Well e sez e was very pleased & was it all in pennies & I told him I <u>was</u> strong but not as strong as that, so e laughs. I tell him that it is the law of Society that none of us is allowed by Ferguson to show our faces in Public so e sez e quite understands – Well e rings the bell for is clerk & in she comes – Now she was pleece becos she larphed at me, but I take no notice & goes on torking to the gent who I've got well away orf with by this time - ..we torks of the mill & e sez it is one of the most treasured possessions of the Trust – Well at that I beams & I sez I'll tell Ferguson & e sez 'moind you do' – Then e asks me if I've seen the mill – I said all the Gang ad, & e sez e opes we are pleased with it too – I sez we are – He sez e & the staff always are very pleased when they get a letter from the gang – Well then the receipt come & I sez good by & all good things to the Trust from the gang & e sez good bye & all good things to the Gang from the Trust - so we shakes and & part, & I walks quick in case the police see me into the taxi – All the Trust looks out of the window to try & see me take orf my mask – but I am ready for them & keep it on – so off we go, & that is the end.

This first instalment caused the press to start taking an interest and catapulted the Gang into the public eye. In February the Daily Mail and Daily Sketch loudly proclaimed 'Masked Woman's £100 Gift in Silver' and 'Gang with good heart – Masked Women's Gift of a Bag full of Silver' bringing Red Biddy to everyone's attention. The Times praised the 'benevolent gangsters' and The Western Morning News and Daily Gazette heralded 'Red Biddy's gift to National Trust'.

In addition to these favourable reports the Evening News tried to uncover who the maidens behind the masks were. Their scurrilous report caused consternation within the Gang at their March meeting.

Fifth meeting – 26th March 1933
Everyone was present

The Gang assembled on the grind stone and Bill proposed a vote of welcome to Lord Beershop after a prolonged illness. In fact Lord Beershop would suffer increasingly from a rare form of anaemia.

Kate and Red Biddy gave their reports of the first drop and they read through the press coverage of the Gang. One article was the Evening News, which attempted the unmasking of the Gang, and it was recorded that suspicion attached to Red Biddy as the informant. They planned the next delivery of money and someone suggested it would be fun to attach £50 notes to miniature bottles of various liqueurs.

The collection for the Roman amphitheatre fund for Chester was £1 but they decided not to visit as it was temporarily closed.

Buoyed up by the success of the Shalford Mill purchase, Bill Stickers suggested the Gang took a look at The Old Court House, Newtown on the Isle of Wight; Kate meanwhile wanted them to look at more water mills in Shropshire. This interest in water mills was as a result of the SPAB campaign with the Daily Mail and The Times to highlight the irreversible decline in the number of water mills left in England.

There is a poignant note in the record book regarding The Artichoke's straightened finances; the Gang resolved that

36

Red Biddy should convey their willingness to take over the rental of the whole mill if he found he was no longer able to afford to keep it. At the time The Artichoke and the Wife to the Artichoke were renting the mill as their weekend cottage.

The meeting concluded with the resolution 'That the Gang may adjourn for other business'.

Sixth meeting – 18th June 1933
All members present

The meeting began as usual on the grind stone; however they were forced to move into the 'Cell' as a large sum of money had to be unpacked and counted.

During the financial statement Bill presented £1 from Erb the Smasher and Kate gave 'a lot of pennies' from her old gentlemen. At this time Kate was working as a housekeeper at one of the grand hotels in London and the gentlemen probably refers to the donations from residents and visiting club members.

The business of the meeting saw the Gang sadly turning down the opportunity to buy the millpond field of 12 acres from the Pious Yudhishthira for £800 but were gladdened by Mr Colenutt's letter announcing Sir John Simeon's willingness to sell The Court House in the Isle of Wight as long as the adjoining field, which had once been the Market Place, was also procured. A visit for all the Gang to inspect The Court House (later to be known as the Old Town Hall) was organised for July.

The letter to the National Trust requesting the right to rent the mill room at Shalford Mill was drafted (as outlined at the beginning of this chapter); however there had been a somewhat acrimonious debate previously over how the Gang should use their new HQ and the Trust's policy in relation to this. Red Biddy wanted to use it for enjoyment and entertaining purposes; Bill, Ag and Kate wanted exclusiveness while Lord Beershop abstained from the argument. In the end the mill ended up being a curious mix of HQ, refuge and rendezvous point for the Gang members.

The second drop of money for the mill was due imminently and they accepted Erb the Smasher's offer with alacrity for him to deliver the booty at the end of the year.

The meeting was concluded with the resolution 'That the Gang do now go and roast the chicken for its lunch'.

The Town Hall of Newtown or Franchville, Isle of Wight – purchased and restored by the Gang for £1,400

It was while Bill Stickers was visiting Black Maria that the Town Hall was brought to her attention. It was purchased from Sir John Simeon for £5 together with the adjoining field for £100. There is short description of the building in the Boo:

'Bill Stickers took note of this ancient building in July 1933. It was built by public subscription in 1699, and is partly stone and partly brick. It has two windows in the North end and four in one side wall, all round-headed in the William and Mary style, and has also at one end a portico with pillars and at the other a double flight of steps and a platform. It is 20 feet by 30 or thereabouts. It consists of a large arguing room with a basement, a loft and some small partitioned lobbies.

'It stands in a field that used to be the market place and contains a pond which appears on ancient maps. It is in very unspoilt surroundings, commanding a view of the Solent and the creek of Newtown. Beside it is the old inn whose sign is the town's seal DE FRENCHVILLE DE LILLE. The town used to be the capital of the island. It was called Franchville. After being sacked by the Danes and the French it never recovered and is today obsolete and derelict.

....

'Mr Colenutt obtained the promise of the building for £5 from Sir John Simeon and also persuaded the owner of the field to sell it for £100. The Artichoke surveyed the Town Hall for the National Trust and advised them to accept it. On estimating that the entire charges would be about £1000 he would have frightened Bill off but for the action of BLACK MARIA who immediately guaranteed the money, whereon Mr Hamer the Secretary of the National Trust agreed to advance the money. The building is very derelict and almost past repair but the Artichoke says he can do it. He will assist and advise Mr Troke a little

38

Artichoke of small experience but great enthusiasm, who surveyed this place of his own free will five years ago.'

During this year Joshua Bottle-Washer wrote three times to the Gang, each recorded in the Boo, purporting to send greetings and felicitations from Ferguson. The first letter thanked Bill for her commendable work on working to save the Old Town Hall, which Kate O'Brien and Lord Beershop had both reported on. The second letter, written from Felsted, is in code and talked about 'flowers, purple and yellow, summer 10-12 feet succeeded by scarlet berries, China'. No-one outside the Gang has managed to crack the code.

In the third letter Joshua Bottle-Washer wrote to Bill Stickers on behalf of herself, Jerry Boham and Sam presenting thanks from Ferguson for all of the Gang's hard work. Within the letter Joshua enclosed 6/3d silver bullion which was to be used for the old Cross (namely Whiteleaf Cross) and the rest for the Old Town Hall.

Whiteleaf Cross Preservation Scheme - £1

The Gang supported the appeal on CS Lewis' recommendation after he had viewed the site with his old friend. Whiteleaf Cross itself, which dominates the local landscape, is a mystery to many. The first reference was in 1738 and the earliest known drawing of it is in the Bodleian library entitled 'Crux Saxonica' dated 1742. By the Enclosure Act 9 of George IV it was declared to be public property. Whiteleaf Hill is another Nature Reserve and has a Neolithic barrow from which burial artefacts from 6,000 years ago have been unearthed. One particular tomb, excavated by Sir William Lindsay Scott in the 1930s, has a man ceremonially buried about 5500 years ago. Whiteleaf Fields (of 62 acres) was acquired from Dr Roger N Goodman.

The National Trust's 1934 Annual Report notes that two residents bought the land below Whiteleaf Cross in the Chilterns, which helped to make the view from that eminence one of the finest in England. These two could not hold the land immune from the spectre of builders for more than a year. The National

Trust took to hold the land if the Whiteleaf Cross Committee were able to buy it.

During the summer Erb and Fred were married at Fred's parish church in Herefordshire, enthusiastically supported by the Gang. Upon their return from honeymoon discussions around the final payment for Shalford Mill increased. This time the Gang rounded up monies from their conscripted members, forcing them to provide the necessary payments and the newly married Erb undertook to make the drop.

4*th* November 1933 - Report of Erb the Smasher
Final Payment for Shalford Mill

I as to report that I got your parcel…alrite and I goes round in ther mercy to the address you says and leaves the mercy beind another car to one side and obscures the numbers, and goes and rings the bell I didn't now wich but guesses and ther elderly bimedelled meniel finds me wearing the marsk and says are you from the gang and I says ah! I must see the secretary personal, and e says alrite and he goes and sees and then e arsks me to cum along and I cums, and I gets so nervious my finger shakes on ther trigger and my gun nearly goes orf and e'd ave called the cops but it doesn't and I ands im ther paper and ther boodle and I arsks if I can smoke a feg and e says yes and e's glad to see me and e rings ther bell and a tiperiper comes in and I as them both covered and I says I want a receipt afore I gives them ther boodle and they gives it me and also a tract wot I send you now and then I suddenly makes my getaway before they knows wots wot and I'm down Victoria Street doing 80 and thats my story and i ope its alrite….

This dramatic drop of the money once again caused a media furore; The Times and The Morning Post both ran the headlines 'Ferguson's Gang – Another gift of £200 to the National Trust' and 'The "Ferguson Gang" – further gift of £200 for beauty spot'. The Daily Express described the Gang as 'a group of anonymous philanthropists' while another paper declared they were 'a gang of humourists'. The Daily Sketch was less sympathetic; its caustic headline 'Ferguson's Gang busy

40

again – Mystery Band with Terrible Names Complete Endowment of Beauty Sport' was followed up in the article with the dismissive sentence: 'This time the representative of Ferguson's Gang sent up his card as though he were a commercial traveller'. Hardly a glowing epithet for the Gang's hard work.

Seventh meeting – 17th December 1933
White Biddy is present, Red Biddy is not and Lord Beershop is absent

The meeting was opened with Bill reading out the letters patient (signed by Ferguson and witnessed by Jerry Boham and Joshua Bottle-Washer) who gave Bill the right of authority. 'I do hereby confer, invest and endow upon in and with Bill Stickers power to act as my deputy legate and plenipotentiary and do instruct Ferguson's Gang to regard Im as such on the occasion of the formal opening of Ferguson's Gang Headquarters.'

This time when the Gang assembled on the grind stone they had another new ritual. 'Ferguson or his plenipotentiary shall advance as far as the door of the room, and thus address the Gang:

Ferguson: Ale Gang

Gang: Ale Ferguson

Ferguson: Is Ferguson's Gang satisfied that this room is a fit and proper place for its ead1/4s?

Gang: It is satisfied

Ferguson: Doth any person within or without this room challenge the right of Ferguson's Gang 2 take this room 4 its ead1/4s?

(There will in all probability be no reply. This is correct.)

Ferguson: I do there4 claim this room as the ead1/4s of Ferguson's Gang, and with the power of the Secular Arm I open this room.

(Ferguson will then open the door)

Ferguson: Ale room

Gang: Ale room

(Ferguson shall then precede the Gang in2 the room)'

Special credit was given to Agatha, Biddy and Kate for their work in raising the £300 by the Gang; 5s from Ferguson and 11s from Lord Beershop. They enjoyed Erb the Smasher's report and the collected press cuttings and gave a hearty vote of thanks.

There was obviously a new scheme being considered as they talked about the impossibility of arranging an expedition for the new undertaking but it is not expanded upon to give any more detail.

In preparation for the seasonal festivities Uncle Gregory had proposed a lino-cut Christmas card design for the Gang to use; it was accepted and a list of people whom they wanted to send the cards to was drawn up.

1934

After the excitement of the previous two years, where the Gang had managed to save two properties, the routine of the girls' lives was once again disrupted. Sister Agatha was offered a role out in Australia to set up an Almoner's training course in Melbourne while Red Biddy, rather daringly for the time, moved in with her lover Luigi Cocuzzi.

Eighth meeting – 4th February 1934
Only Lord Beershop, Sister Agatha and Bill Stickers present

Eighth meeting – 4th February 1934
Only Lord Beershop, Sister Agatha and Bill Stickers present

To banish any winter blues they devised yet another new ritual; this time Lord Beershop entered the HQ followed by Sister Agatha (Is Aconite) bearing an 'oly spoon and Bill Stickers bearing an 'oly wine glass. They sat on the new mercy seat embroidered by Bill; in later life Bill would become a Guinness Book of Records holder for her embroidery works.

Having cleaned the rooms they then settled down to a lunch of: York ham, poached eggs and new potatoes; a dessert of toast and cream cheese, followed by bananas accompanied with Imperial Tokey 1883; this wine was considered 'the wine of Kings and the king of wines' due to the high regard given by the 18th century French Court. It was also a favourite of the Russian Imperial Court and goes to show the Gang enjoyed the best of everything.

The Gang partook of an afternoon siesta after lunch and then the meeting officially began; there is an interesting comment regarding Red Biddy. 'A resolution of resigned regret at the decease of Red Biddy was then passed, and a hearty clap given to her ghost'. In fact the demise of Red Biddy was due to her engagement; she reappears first as White Biddy (as in her impending wedding) and then Shot Biddy (after her marriage in November 1934 as in 'shot of parents').

The Gang produced 7/6 for the Sullington Warren appeal in West Sussex but failed to organise an expedition to the Old Town Hall. Agatha raised a concern about the relationship with the National Trust being too informal; the imminent retirement of Mr Hamer, the Secretary, brought this issue to a head, so the Gang decided that a formal written agreement reflecting the financial obligations of both parties should be sought.

Sullington Warren Purchase Scheme – 7/6 donation

Sullington Warren was close to Bill Sticker's and Poolcat's Surrey homes; it was somewhere that Poolcat would regularly walk across on his long rambles. It was a heathland of mixed wet and dry areas supporting a wide variation of plants and birds. The National Trust appeal needed to raise £1,740 for the 28 acres in order to save the nine prehistoric round barrows (which are all now listed as Ancient Monuments and as such come under the protection of English Heritage).

The 1935 report wrote: 'The National Trust heartily endorses the Appeal now on foot to save from 'development' 29 acres of Sullington Warren, which is regarded as one of the finest places of natural beauty in West Sussex'.

Ninth meeting: 16th-17th March 1934
Kate O'Brien not present

Unusually this meeting was not held at the Gang's HQ, instead the planned expedition to the Isle of Wight was finally to take place and to ensure they were able to make an early start they stayed overnight at Sister Agatha's. They started with an excellent dinner at Café Royal before retiring to Sister Agatha's Cell for an enjoyable evening. They held the same opening ritual; Lord Beershop inducted with the 'oly oil, 'oly Ring and 'oly Croque.

As they counted out the Victorian silver they had collected in taxes, they drank damson gin and Lord Beershop danced the evening away in 'Is liturgical boots' before they finally retired for the evening.

The next day all of the Gang, except White Biddy, then set out to Waterloo and caught the 9.50am train to Ryde. Arriving there Black Maria's chauffeur drove them to Newtown so that the Gang could carefully inspect the Old Town Hall which was in a state of disrepair and full of workmen's ladders. Lord Beershop had brought the 'oly oil to anoint the building and Bill Stickers was called upon to address the building on behalf of the Gang; what the workmen made of this spectacle is unrecorded. Before leaving they investigated the surrounding fields and applauded the scenery which 'was enhanced by the tide being well up in the creek'.

Black Maria's chauffeur collected them and took them back to 'The Ghost House' where Black Maria entertained them. Lord Beershop unfortunately had to leave to catch the 4.55pm train home but the others remained as house guests to enjoy dinner and spend a comfortable night on the island.

Tenth meeting: 5th May 1934
Tenth meeting: 5th May 1934
All present except White Biddy
The £2 10s raised by the Gang was mostly sent by Ferguson; they also had £40 0s 4d in the bank.

The highlight of the evening was the dinner being cooked by Bill and Kate on the Gang's new oven; a Kubex (a camping oven which sat on a gas ring) and a Riffingille cooker (the world renowned oil based stove made in Aston, Birmingham) and they ate with relish the dinner of roast duck and new potatoes with junket and cream for pudding.

The financial overruns by the builders at the Old Town Hall were obviously prominent in their thoughts. Someone raised the question of how this occurred. The Gang understood from The Artichoke that the serious increase in their estimate costs was due partly to the builders' inexperience (who were enthusiastic to work on the project but had very little historical restoration experience) and were not necessarily receptive to the SPAB methods. The Artichoke was carefully monitoring the builders' proceedings – and for this the Gang were particularly grateful.

There had been some discussion about what the Old Town Hall should be used for. One proposal was for the Youth Hostel Association (YHA) to use it; the YHA movement was enthusiastically endorsed by both Trevelyan and Williams-Ellis and this would have held substantial significance for the Gang. The members endorsed the proposal put forward for the place to be fitted out for the YHA as not only would the building be regularly used but it would also be available to the Gang if they ever wanted to stay!

They finished the meeting with a collection to subscribe money to the testimonial to Mr Hamer for his retirement as Secretary of the National Trust.

Extraordinary meeting – Worshiping the four colours of the dawn: 1ˢᵗ July 1934

The Gang were intensely interested in the spiritual world and the water ley lines associated with ancient beliefs. To this end Lord Beershop had drawn a detailed plan of the water sources around the Shalford Mill (still on display at the Mill today) providing the Gang with a map of where they could go on 'oly X. Cursions to collect water samples from the underground tributaries of the River Thames.

During the July meeting Lord Beershop, Bill Stickers and Sister Agatha stayed overnight at the HQ to celebrate the spiritual world. As the stroke of midnight could be heard ringing out from the parish church bell the three members assembled together in the 'Chamber of Horrors' and swore in deathly tones 'That at whatever cost i 4 1 will uphold Ferguson's Gang' as they placed their hands on the 'oly croque.

As the moon drew clear from the trees and they waited for the first cock's crow, Agatha and Bill made coffee on their stove, stealing out into the darkness to raid the farm for milk. Then as the first sign of light became visible Lord Beershop threw

45

open the dawn window and, in the presence of a shining Venus and Capella, the Gang watched the slowly rising sun.

The four o'clock chimes carried across the summer air, Lord Beershop and Bill disrobed and leapt into the Tillingbourne River, enjoying the refreshing feel of the water; splashing around before getting out and drying off. As the rays of the morning light broke through Lord Beershop conferred a knighthood on Bill with the words 'Rise up Bill Stickers of the Tyburn' and on Agatha with the words 'Rise up Dame Annis the Clear, of the Turnmil'; in return Agatha and Bill conferred the Title of Westbourne onto Lord Beershop in addition to all the other titles held. These three titles completed the adulation of The Thames by containing the names of its tributaries.

21st July 1934 - Report of Ferguson's Secretary Jerry Boham National Trust AGM
Sire

I july attended the Annular Metinge of the Natural truss and beg 2 rep O as follows, wiz:-

There wos a grate and reppryhensible gathering ov lorabiding and seed8 sitysens ov orl seckses and I tuk an unnotised sete were I cud se and ear. The bloke in the chare was a nice gent a Lord Zetland & there wos other lauds in a roe saif behind a table, but they woant drest up & no crownds, and nobody thru nothing at them.

Lord Z made a gud speech about the years work. E thank awl those good euonymous bennyfactors oo ad elped the truss and among them those eunomanimities oo chuse to ide under the naim of Ferguson's Gang at wich ther wos a pleesd teetur went round the Awl shoing ow your Gang Sire is none and depreshiated. E wos very strong on the suxess of the new cunninig & complykated skeem wich the truss comity as thort out for saving the laix wich was in pearl. E didnt seme ankshus but wot the 7500 lbs still wanted wud come in easy like. E didn't menshun the ole town all nor the ole witless cross.

Then mister Amer ad is leavin gift made in a few choice words. It tuk the form ov 2 W.C. pictures of the laix and a check. (N.B. the pictures stood behind the tabil one each side of the bus

46

of Q. Victoria but I dont think the buss was giv away).[2] (E sed e should spend the check as e dam well liked and get things e wanted and e sed e mite even be abil to offer to join Fergusons Gang if they would have him.)[1] (Mr Amer made a feline and a numerous reply and wos most populous.) And e told the nu secretary e shud jolly well chivvy him. Then anuther lawd, the markis of loathing maid a long speech but so good that I kep awake tho 2 prone to go to sleep at metings. E wants the truss to enlarge its spear so as to take over the larger & smaller houses of the old ordure wich is disappearing, & e maid a good bizness propersishun ov it. I think umbly Sire that Bill ad better not be toald this or e may go orf the deep end & come and dere Winsor Carsol or Catsworf or Nole as the Gangs Contribushun to the skeme. Anyway Bill will probly rede about it in the Times if e blues 2d.

Then it was past 5 and we wanted T but there wos a crool discussion on bludy spawts on truss property but i didn't lissen much & egged up to the t tabel for the rush wen it began. There wos a lord ov one of the laix spok against the idear. E was fine to luk at, most like a lawd ov enny, and sloe and dignified. E as such a fine voice that e wos wunce speker for barleymint. The bludsupporters didn't get their weigh.

End of offishal repought. Sined by the secrotery Jerry Boham.

1st October 1934 - Report of Kate O'Brien The Nark
Deposit for the Town Hall

Now the report.

I took the goat, documents and card in the car this afternoon, collected my father as escort, called at Harrods for a mask, then drove to the Trust.

I was shown into the room we last saw Hamer in. The new secretary is a nice bloke, he was v charming & said it was an agreeable surprise as he hadnt expected such a big cheque so soon. (Receipt enclosed). He asked about our feelings re youth hostel V. Museum. I raised the points we had discussed, i.e.

Curator and heat, & he quite agreed & said he had asked them if they had thought of that. The local committee apparently hadnt.

....Our cards work lovely, no waiting. I dont wonder he was impressed with the goat, I ad never seen such another.

Once again the daring drop of the money made headline news. The Daily Mail, Daily Telegraph and Daily Sketch all reported: 'Masked Woman gives £500 – Aid for National Trust'. The Daily Mail went on to say: 'The 'gang' is believed to be a body of ten men and women interested in the preservation of beauty spots and historic places'. How surprised their readers would have been if The Times had been able to reveal the true identity of the Gang.

Eleventh meeting: 11th October 1934 held at Lord Beershop's Palace
Present: Ferguson, Lord Beershop, Bill Stickers and White Biddy

At this time Sister Agatha had left to go to Australia which accounts for her absence from this point going forward. The members present discussed the £900 that remained to be 'found' for the Isle of Wight project and joked that they would soon have 'stepping stones all around England'. There was an eager anticipation towards a new adventure being started soon, and much talk about the Gang's banquet at 'Florences' to celebrate their tenth anniversary. There is no indication if Florence's relates to a person, restaurant or family home, however there is a possibility it relates to Florence Dugdale, Thomas Hardy's second wife, who was a friend of White Biddy.

Sister Agatha's absence was acknowledged in true Gang style. There was a minute's silence during which White Biddy, as her oldest friend, burst into tears.

Dovedale Appeal - £20 donation

Kate O'Brien petitioned for support of this appeal; having attended school near here the area had strong memories for her. Much of this dale is now owned by the National Trust. Hall Dale and Hurts Wood (113 acres) acquired on 1st January

48

1934 from Robert McDougall and land at Lode Mill (47 acres) was acquired on 11th November 1934 from Elizabeth Prince and Lloyds Bank Ltd. Successive properties were added until 1938 then finally Wolfscote Dale was added in 1948 forming the South Peak Estate.

After having lived together Red Biddy and Luigi finally became married; they attended the Chelsea Registry Office with a handful of friends on 10th November to quietly make their wedding vows. There was no time, or money, for a honeymoon though; a week later Red Biddy was attending the Gang's meeting.

Twelfth meeting: 18th November 1934
This time Kate was present but Sister Agatha was still absent

Their financial boodle for the meeting totalled £70 11s with another goat being expected (probably their slang for a bob or shilling). They resolved that the next adventure should be for an open space rather than a building; this may have something to do with the bad experience of the spiralling building costs at the Old Town Hall.

There had obviously been some fraught correspondence with Mr Colenutt regarding the Old Town Hall being used by the YHA. Bill reported that he was being extremely contentious and 'threatening us with legal cartridges'.

Colenutt's attitude riled Kate sufficiently for her to declare that if they made the Old Town Hall into a museum then she would begin a personal crusade to make 'a public stink and fight them'. The rest of the Gang shared the sentiment but hoped that Professor Trevelyan would prove a match for Colenutt. For note: although the YHA would have the building for a short while, fate would conspire against the Gang and the Old Town Hall would eventually end up as a museum; it now houses the National Trust's exhibitions, one of which is a dedicated homage to Ferguson's Gang.

With Agatha still away the Gang's resolution was 'That the Gang do now write a letter to Sister Agatha' presumably to keep her updated on the projects and plans.

The next meeting was scheduled for December and it was suggested that Silent O'Moyle (Kate's father) be approached to see if he would make the next mystery drop of booty to the National Trust.

The meeting concluded with a tasty dinner of roast duck, potatoes and half an onion with trifle as a dessert and finished off with biscuits and cheese.

Thirteenth meeting: 16th December 1934
Both Kate and Sister Agatha absent

The meeting was held at the HQ but neither Kate nor Agatha were present. The records show that Silent O'Moyle was in receipt of the goat (booty) which they had split down into £100 'Kids'. The use of caprine terminology came from Bill's recent venture into goat breeding; Silent was due to deliver the money to the Trust the next day. The use of coinage was obviously causing more and more risk and they wondered about changing the Gang's bank account into the name of Ferguson's Gang so they could simply issue an anonymous cheque when securing properties for the National Trust.

Once again the Gang sent Christmas cards, agreeing to prioritise Mr Hamer, Silent O'Moyle and the Advisers (Lord Beershop's parents), and to include photographs of the Mill and Old Town Hall in Hamer's card.

The resolution for the meeting was 'That the Gang do now get its lunch ready'; they cooked braised pheasant, with chestnuts and sausages, and green figs and cream for pudding. This dinner was voted the best dinner they had cooked so far. In fact they went so far as to the record the recipe for posterity:

1 pheasant
½ lb chestnuts
½ lb chipolata sausages
1 carrot, turnip and onion
1 dessertspoonful barley

Fry pheasant brown with sausages and onion. Blanch and peel chestnuts and cut vegetables into dice. Put all in a casserole with a little water and cook very gently for two hours.

17th December 1934 - Report of Silent O'Moyle
Payment for Old Town Hall

The delivery of the 5 £100 kidds by Silent O'Moyle.

3.30. Dusk. The Beershop looks at Silent O'Moyle. Silent nods; they go out. Outside they get into a taxi & give the driver Buckkingum Pallice Gdns. Silent puts on is mask, turns up is coller, pulls down is at and sits, silent. The Taxi stops at no.10. The Beershop waits in it; Silent O'Moyle gets out, e don't say a word, e vanishes into no.7. There is sumthing in is and....

....Silent walks into no.7; he speaks no word; he enters the Secretary's room; he is alone. The Secretary is engaged.

Silent seizes his chance. Is he observed? He searches the room inch by inch: no perricks there.

The Secretary enters: Silent has his finger on his lip. The Goat is safely and silently delivered.

The Secretary longs for a word: he fetches in his underling – a chatty lad – but Silent's finger is on his lip. In exchange for a receipt Silent leaves the Bottle of Poison and smiles irradiate the Secretarial Countenances. Then silently Silent absconds. The deed is done, and Silent sinks into the arms of the anxious B.B.

The press reaction to Silent O'Moyle's drop was mixed; The People sensationalised the drop. 'Red Biddy and her Gang are at it again – Scotland Yard Knows it!'. The article starts: '"The Yard," they say, has "cleaned up" gangland in London; driven the gang leaders out of the country; made the West End safe for every citizen. But HAS IT?

'There is one powerful gang which still flourishes under the very nose, so to speak, of Lord Trenchard!'

The Times and The Telegraph were more restrained but both reported the 'Masked Gang' visiting the National Trust. The Morning Post though took the Gang more seriously; they began to rally their readers in support of the Gang's ethos against urbanisation. 'The proposal to erect modern bungalows on the parkland of Camilla Lacey is only one instance of the desecration of the countryside which is going on throughout England. We shall surely go down to posterity as a generation of vandals comparable to the "Reformers" who spoiled the churches... The Government does nothing; the amenity societies lack funds. Has not the time come to raise a troop of militants who will agitate until they rob the despoiler of his prey? The idea may be commended to the unidentified zealots known as 'Ferguson's Gang'.'

1935

Once again the personal lives of the Gang members were in a torrid flux; Kate O'Brien left the busy world of hoteliers and became a housekeeper at the same school as Isabelle Granger. Sister Agatha returned later in the year from Australia and resumed the tumultuous relationship with Jervis-Read. Red Biddy failed her final medical degree exams, forcing her to leave King's College without qualifying and Bill Stickers began to be involved with the CPRE as well as the National Trust.

Bill persuaded a number of landowners about the benefits of donating land to the National Trust in order to save the coastal area; she was involved in saving Predannack and Lansallos (which the Gang went on to also donate money to). Perhaps her greatest work with the CPRE was purchasing the remainder of Mr Whiting's property from his executors, thus ensuring the whole plot surrounding Coneysburrow Cove was presented to the National Trust.

The Great Banquet of the National Trust – 28th February 1935

The annual dinner of the National Trust had the great and the good present. The Prince of Wales was present as the speaker and he eloquently eulogised the need to support the National Trust in preserving our countryside.

As at the previous National Trust dinners the Gang decided on masked disguises. Dressed again in black velvet Bill Stickers and Shot Biddy went to Black Maria's London 'Hole' ready to meet the others. They were joined a short while later by Lord Beershop, Ferguson, Kate O'Brien and Silent O'Moyle. Ferguson and Silent had selected to disguise themselves as 'the upper classes'; the other two were a little more conspicuous.

Lord Beershop wore a flamboyant outfit of Cardinal's Robes while Kate had ingeniously created a disguise with loopholes that would allow it to be swiftly removed if she needed a speedy getaway during the evening.

The Gang made their way to Park Lane and headed into the Dorchester where they 'cased the joint'. Black Maria led the way, ably assisted by Kate who had made a careful reconnaissance of the hotel's layout before the event.

Seizing a valuable table, aided and abetted by The Artichoke, the Gang settled down for the dinner which went well except that Kate's monkey got into the soup and afterwards threw the ice cream about. Kate's monkey is mentioned elsewhere in the Boo but whether it was a pet or a reference to her temperament cannot be established.

After HRH The Prince of Wales' speech, Lord Zetland, Chairman of the National Trust, paid homage to the Trust's benefactors and then went on '2 throw a deeply appreciated bouquet to 'those cheery modern counterparts of Robin Hood – Ferguson's Gang'.'

This sent the neighbouring table into giggles, clearly amused by the Gang; the Boo notes they 'jurks their thumbs and mutters 'that's them'.' This was noticed by Silent who tried to divert attention by using the 'deaf and dumb language' – presumably a swift hand gesture. Towards the end of the evening 'an old female perrick' getting out of a lift recognised them, however the Gang managed to promptly escape although not all went empty-handed. Shot Biddy managed to pinch the Dorchester's entire supply of toothpicks – providing the Gang with a valuable ransoming tool to raise funds with!

Buttermere Appeal - £1 donation

When the Buttermere appeal was launched the Gang wholeheartedly supported it, the proximity to Professor Trevelyan's aristocratic family home meant they felt a certain loyalty to him in ensuring the site was saved. The area was most famous for local inhabitant Mary Robinson in the 18th century who was known as the Maid of Buttermere, later the subject of a novel by Melvyn Bragg. Crummock Water (1,018.78 acres) was acquired on 7th July 1935 from WMW Marshall; the lake is one and quarter miles long and half a mile wide.

14th meeting: 3rd March 1935
Held at Gang HQ. Present: Silent O'Moyle (representing Ferguson), Lord Beershop, Bill Stickers, Kate O'Brien and Shot Biddy

Before the meeting could get started Shot Biddy surprised the Gang by producing a magnificent silver cup which she 'had lifted' from the Dorchester banquet. Her outlandish activities won her a hearty clap for the great and brilliant crime. This daring act of robbery sealed her position as an acclaimed member of the inner circle of Ferguson's Gang. The cup still sits in residency at Shalford Mill.

The financial statements of the meeting were boosted by the 'compulsory conscriptions' of £200 from Black Maria. £293 2s 0d in the bank and £25 12s 6d raised by the Gang through levies.

The final instalment for the Old Town Hall was due and as they discussed the drop Lord Beershop suggested Uncle Gregory as the nominated deliverer which was fully endorsed by the rest of the Gang.

The work in the Old Town Hall was coming to an end so the Gang was eager to see the finished building. They discussed a proposed expedition to Newtown and provisionally fixed the date for the 12th May. Kate was made responsible for organising the motor to take them down with Bill making the other necessary arrangements for the Gang's travel. The meeting ended with the resolution 'That the Gang do now lay the table 4 its lunch'.

The lunch cooked and served to their guest was braised chicken with green beans and a dessert of green figs and cream. Later, having eaten, Shot Biddy swore herself in on the mill shaft and was '4mally aspersed' by Lord Beershop.

15th *meeting: 12th May 1935*
All present except Sister Agatha who was still away

The monies due to the National Trust were to be delivered the next day. Unfortunately Uncle Gregory's sudden work requirement to go to America meant he was unable to make the drop (he was in fact due to sign contracts with his American publishers); instead Bill was nominated as the drop person instead.

The woods project they had considered was deemed too expensive, costing £5,500 in total; instead the Gang switched to the Bolberry Down Appeal and agreed they would offer to take this over for £900 which they would pay in two years. Whether the Gang actually took over this appeal is unclear. It doesn't feature in their list of sites saved nor do they appear as major benefactors in the Trust's records, it may well be that Bill persuaded the others to focus instead on saving land along the Cornish coast, something she was involved in through her role at CPRE. The saga of how the Old Town Hall should be used continued, the Gang had obviously managed to sway some influence behind the scenes as a letter from the YHA was received. The YHA heartily agreed to the Gang being able to use the Old Town Hall for sojourns and also taking the Gang up on their kind offer to provide some furniture. In keeping with their appreciation of Arts and Crafts and love of traditionally crafted pieces, Kate agreed to speak to a craftsman who still 'employed the old ways' and would make an oak table with dovetail joints rather than the modern way of using screws and nails.

At half past ten in the morning, the Gang left their HQ and set off in Kate's car to the Isle of Wight. Kate and Lord Beershop shared the driving and the day was bright and sunny although there was a hint of a chill wind in the air.

They stopped for lunch in a secluded beech wood sitting amongst a carpet of bluebells and Solomon's seal. In the distance a cuckoo could be heard calling to a mate. They feasted on a glorious alfresco picnic of chicken mousse, Russian salad, lychees and cream accompanied by a fine Chateau Larose Blanche.

Catching the 2.30pm ferry they drove directly to Newtown. Lord Beershop, in usual fashion, solemnly blessed the building before the Gang raced inside to inspect the work and to take photographs of the finished building as a keepsake; no doubt pleased that the building was finally completed.

Returning home, they stopped at Cowes in order to partake of afternoon tea; and although there were only four of them they managed to consume five waffles and eight cakes.

They caught the 7.30pm ferry home, tired but buoyed up with the success of the outing; Lord Beershop was overcome with emotion though. Giving a loud joyous yell as they disembarked she charged off the boat and along the stone pier no doubt much to the annoyance of the ferry crew.

Kate and Lord Beershop again took turns driving as night began to fall, returning home after depositing Bill and Biddy at the HQ.

13th May 1935 - Report of Bill Stickers
Final Payment for Old Town Hall

Me and Shot Biddy meets at Silent O'Moyle's and I finds is disguise on the bed and gets in2 it. Biddy ales a taxi and of we goes. I pops in2 the Trust HQ while Biddy and the man covers me. The Porter sez Come In Sir when e seen me card and e looses me in2 the Perrick Room and I waits till Hildebrand and His Son Harlebrand comes in; their ands shake orrible as they count the boodle. They try 2 delay me but I dashes aht wiv the repeat and the taxi man makes a racing getaway. I changes me disguise at Silent's, put on me other, and goes straight back 2 the Trust HQ, 2 make sure i don't lose me nurve.

The media attention once again paid homage to the Gang, building on the Morning Post's stance of 'enough is enough'. As well as The Times, The Morning Post and The News Chronicle carrying the story, The Sunday Pictorial rallied their readers: 'There are also gangsters in England. But I am not referring now to the razor-slashing, racecourse variety, who for long enjoyed an immunity motorists never had, but to the 'Ferguson Gang' who turn up at odd moments with large contributions to the National Trust so as to save our land from becoming one large brick-heap.'

The Gang went on to even greater media heights during that summer. On Sunday 25th August Ferguson, in the guise of his stand-in, Erb the Smasher, made the historic recording. As previously mentioned this gave the National Trust membership figures and funds a vital boost. Hamer, the previous secretary who had recently been awarded 'Commander of the Civil Division of the said Most Excellent Order' had used his family connections to facilitate the BBC appeal.

Erb's clear, persuasive, fervent appeal moved almost a thousand listeners to donate money to the National Trust.

'I am Ferguson of Ferguson's Gang. I appeal to you tonight for the National Trust. That means for the beauty of England; for all that is left of the England that belongs to you and me and is vanishing under our eyes.

'The land held by the National Trust is your land and nobody else's. The cliffs that you buy for the Nation will always be open for you to walk on. Nobody can turn you out of the woods and fields that are held for you by the National Trust. But no Government grant supports the work of the Trust; it is kept going by your efforts and mine. And it urgently needs more subscribing members to help in its battle against the Octopus; the Octopus, whose tentacles, in the shape of jerrybuilt estates and ribbon development, are stretching like a pestilence over the face of England.

'Green grass turning to bricks and dust,
Stately homes will soon go bust;
No defence but the National Trust.

'Do you remember what happened at Stonehenge? ... Do anything but watch the Octopus at work and say 'why doesn't somebody do something about it?'. You can do something yourselves, whetherlike Ferguson's Gang you call at the offices of the Trust in a mask and deposit a sack of bullion, or join the Trust as a subscribing member...'

Riding on the public interest and having completed the two major donations of the Old Mill and Old Town Hall, the Gang continued to donate smaller amounts to the general appeals.

Bill Stickers' love of Cornwall influenced their next two donations to Lansallos and Pentire.

Lansallos Appeal - £3 donation
The land at Fowey was part of Lansallos Barton Farm, Lansallos. 62.22 acres were acquired on 5 May 1936 from JS Andres.

Pentire Appeal - £2 donation
This large tract of land ranged from Pentire Head to Port Quin on Pentire Farm, St Minver, Cornwall. 367 acres were acquired on 12 December 1936 from W M Mollison.

The Gang's love of the natural deities, demonstrated by their interest in Stonehenge and the Four Colours of the Dawn worship, meant that when the Avebury appeal was launched they felt it was essential to save the site. The donation they made reflected this; it was far more significant than the amounts given to the other appeals.

Avebury Appeal - £100 donation
The Gang's love of sacred site worship meant this site held a particularly special place in their hearts. The Neolithic henge monument had three stone circles, one of which was the largest in Europe. During the 1930s the stone circle of Avebury was excavated by archaeologist Alexander Keiller.

As well as the Trust purchasing Avebury Manor Farm (636 acres) acquired on 10th October 1943 from A T Farthing, they also bought from Keiller the Norris Farmland of 248 acres, acquired on 12th December 1943.

Pembroke Appeal - £1 donation
The Gang felt impelled by their friendship with Joshua Bottle-Washer, to support this appeal. Its location was close to Joshua's Welsh weekend home and has the famous Bosherston Lakes which were created 200 years ago to provide a backdrop to Stakepole Court and its wildlife included water birds, dragonflies and otters. It became part of the National Park in 1952.

Having decided to purchase an open tract of land rather than a building which would need restoration, Bill Stickers identified the ideal plot. It was a tract of coastal land in south Cornwall and Bill lobbied hard for the Gang's support; the rock on this site went on to influence her choice of Bardic name.

By purchasing this the Gang saved England's south-westerly extremity and prevented the expansion of the commercial site at Land's End.

Mayon Cliffs, Sennen – purchased and restored by the Gang for £600

Mayon Cliffs was 39 acres at Land's End, which is to the south of the village of Sennen, between the cove and Land's End. Part of this was a rock called the 'Irish Lady' at the north end of Gamper Bay. Legend says it is named in memory of a shipwrecked Irish woman marooned on the windswept rock who could not be rescued and whose ghost is said to appear in stormy weather.

Bill Stickers took the name 'Arlodhes Ywerdhon' (which translates as Irish Lady) when she became a Cornish-language bard, a member of the Cornish Gorsedd. She also composed a song which began:

> Up on the cliffs by Mayon Castle,
> What 'as you seen to make a fuss?
> Up on the cliffs by Mayon Castle,
> There I seen the Octopus.
> What was the Octopus a-doing,
> East of the Longships as you go?
> E'd some bricks and a load o' concrete,
> For to start a bungalow.
> Scarlet bricks and rubbery tiling,
> Bright red boxes all in a row,
> Tin kiosk for the teas and petrol,
> Parkin' place for the cars to go.

The National Trust News of February 1936 gave an update of the Gang's purchase of Sennen: 'They called in the absence of the Secretary and handed over notes to complete the purchase of land near Sennen Cove, in Cornwall. They also left a Christmas present, much enjoyed by the staff, and a Christmas card with their names and the seal of the gang.'

Trevescan Cliffs, Sennen – purchased and restored for £450

The Gang increased the land at Sennen by purchasing a further 16 acres at Trevescan. This new addition ran from Mayon Cliffs to Carn Clog, at Land's End. The purchase money was delivered in secret by the Gang: 'These irrepressible gangsters chose Christmas Eve to carry out yet another raid. Taking every precaution one of them stealthily deposited a suspicious-looking object marked 'Highly pershibale, deliver at once.' On inspection it turned out to be a pastille box. It contained £200. In the pastille box was a picture postcard upon which was inscribed:

'The Liability of Trevescan,
Is paid by Fergusons as e' bes-can,
This 'ere design of fishes
We do enclose with our good wishes.'

This rhyme gave clear indication how the £200 from the mysterious gangsters was to be expended.'

1936-1939

The next few years saw the girls becoming caught up in their own personal adventures; they had less time to meet up and the advent of war was threatening. Bill Stickers took an active role within the Cornish branch of the CPRE where she worked tirelessly to save large areas of Cornish countryside. Red Biddy and Luigi had their first child, a daughter named Karin, and set up their furniture making business. Sister Agatha was finally married to her true-love, Harold Jervis-Read, after he had extracted a divorce from his first wife and Lord Beershop left London, returning to her family's home in Sutton Coldfield.

This activity did not cease all the Gang's activity with the National Trust; they continued to garner support wherever possible. Bill Stickers involved other members of the Gladstone clan in the Gang's work; Mr and Mrs GFG Pollard (herself and Uncle Gregory); Mrs J Gladstone (her mother), Mrs H Gladstone (her cousin's wife) and R Gladstone (her brother) were all listed as having donated money to the National Trust. In fact Waterstone revealed Bill Stickers used a legacy from an elderly aunt to purchase and present Predannack Wartha, Revena and Pennywiligie Points in Lundy Bay. She also employed her persuasive tactics to purchase Rosemullion Head from the Maudsleys (of course using a conscripted supporter's money).

The Gang suffered a set-back when the National Trust decided it was unable to participate in their next project. In September 1938 Sister Agatha wrote to Donald Matheson, Secretary of the National Trust, bringing The Old Pump House at Hunsden to their attention; a property dating from 1497 and which was in danger of being bought by a speculative builder for scrap something that was commonplace at the time. The property was situated in the corner of the village; the main house had six bedrooms and although built in the 15th century had been altered in the 1700s; there were five weather-boarded cottages also dating from the 18th century, a barn and two other cottages which were used for servants; the whole lot was being sold for £2,200.

Although the Gang were short of funds at the time (so unable to purchase it outright), they did guaranteed to pay the rent and rates with a view to repaying the National Trust for the purchase price over a number of years. They extolled the fact that there was an annual income of £120 from the property (made up of £52 for the house and £88 for the cottages – both less rates).

The correspondence (held in the Trust archives) ends a month later when Matheson writes to Bill Stickers to say that although the Trust has inspected the property they do not deem it of significant importance to make it proper for the Trust to hold in permanent preservation for the nation. He does stress that the Trust would support the Gang if they wished to purchase the property themselves and hopes they will not be disappointed by the news.

The Gang were more successful when they discovered an old monastic building on the recommendation of CS Lewis who would often pass by when he went on one of his long rambles through the Oxfordshire villages. Ferguson's Gang went on to purchase and restore the building as their last major property donation.

Priory Cottages, Steventon – purchased and restored for £580

The property had four cottages at Steventon near Abingdon which formed three sides of a small open court. It was part of an older block of timber-framed monastic buildings from the 16th century with three gables on the north-side and two square projecting bay windows, one above the other, with oak mullions and transoms. The original fireplace and panelling had unfortunately already been removed to the Manor House, Sutton Courtenay.

The property once belonged to Westminster Abbey however in the early 1900s it was a residential property lived in by Mrs Langford with her daughter and two sons. The house was seen as a site of historical interest by the historian CRJ Currie who included it within his book 'Smaller Domestic Architecture and Society in North Berkshire, c.1300-c.1650, with special reference to Steventon' in 1976.

As the storm clouds of impending war began to swirl over England, the Gang were forced to relinquish their sole dedication to saving England's heritage. Each took up the new challenge though, becoming involved in vital work which ensured they were at the forefront of the war effort. Bill joined the Women's Land Army, Sister Agatha enlisted with the Red Cross, Lord Beershop became an ambulance driver and Red Biddy helped to rescue refugees from Germany. Once again the Gang were united in their efforts to save England.

Part 2: Tracking down the Gang

Chapter Six: Unmasking the Maidens

The attempts to unmask this mob of maidens have been protracted and sporadic, lasting over eighty years. Apart from the Boo there is little centrally collated information on the Gang; yet their dedication to supporting the National Trust cannot be underestimated. The illusion the five girls created has intrigued for almost a century and attempts to identify their real personas began soon after they were formed. The first attempt was undertaken by the Evening News in 1932 which used an inside informant to provide character summaries but failed to winkle out any names. The reporter gave some in-depth descriptions of the Gang members which, although elaborate and illuminating, were not always entirely accurate. The published description was:

'The 'gang' was formed by a young Society woman who, after a brilliant career at Cambridge University came to King's College and banded her friends together under the name of the 'Ferguson Gang'. She is the grand-daughter of an Earl whose name is one of the best known in the land. It is nothing like Ferguson!

'Her husband is a well-known author, and they live in one of the prettiest spots in Devonshire.

'**Good by Stealth:** There are now five young Society women in the 'gang'. One is almoner at one of the largest hospitals, and another is 'housekeeper' at a West End hotel. Each is devoted to the preservation of British beauty spots, and they use some of their money to this end.'

It was another forty years before another clue was provided, although thankfully this one was a little more illuminating. Sir Clough Williams-Ellis in his autobiography *Architect Errant*, published in 1971, revealed who had initiated the creation of Ferguson's Gang. It was one of his good friends, who he had edited a book for, and he wrote the words 'Peggy herself at last confessed and gave me leave to reveal, though I have become privy to other equally anonymous and beneficent ploys that are still under the seal of secrecy'. This at least provided a Christian name for one of the Gang.

The next citation, a quarter of the century after Williams-Ellis, came in an obituary published in The Independent in 1996; this revealed that Margaret Pollard was Bill Stickers, part of the Gladstone political dynasty. The obituary had been written by Ann Trevenen Jenkin a fellow Cornish-language bard of Bill Stickers; their friendship explains the intimate detail Jenkin was able to provide about Bill Sticker's life that had not been made public before.

Jenkin retold how Bill Stickers had published *Bewnans Alysaryn* in 1941, a pastiche on the ancient Cornish Miracle Plays, one of the main sources for modern Cornish. Carader, the first Grand Bard, called it an important work in 'Dasserghyans Kernewek', the 'revival of Cornish'. Bill Stickers was also the Gorsedd harpist for many years, playing a small Irish harp.

In the homily Bill was praised for being an intellectual and romantic idealist who was also intensely practical; an expert embroiderer, an authority on goats and a worker for the conservation of Cornwall.

Jenkin's description provided a huge step forward; there was now a real name to work with even if there was no hint of who Bill's fellow conspirators were. Further clues were discovered at the beginning of the new Millennium. The National Trust magazine article (from Spring 2008) by Sue Herdman provided further information on other gang members; giving details for the Head of the Gang, three of the inner-circle members and one of their loyal supporters.

'We know that the Lord Beershop had been an art student at the Slade and was the gang's official artist. Red Biddy (named for her Communist leanings) had been a brigadier's daughter, became a doctor, saw the inside of prison and was noted for her disinterest in soap and water.

'Sister Agatha, the gang's organiser, gave astonishingly good teas and was noted for her vivacious, no-nonsense manner. There was no actual Ferguson, although a male friend occasionally assumed his identity. It was he who made an inspirational BBC radio broadcast on behalf of the gang in 1935, appearing in the studio in dinner jacket and mask. It netted 600 new members and £900 in contributions.

'Another ally was The Artichoke, aka John Macgregor, a well-known conservation architect. He came into contact with the gang when they donated the derelict Shalford Mill in Surrey, of which he became the tenant.'

Concurrently the publication of Juliet Gardiner's book 'The Thirties – an intimate history' published in 2010, gave the final clue. Her chapter on 'Accommodating the Octopus' contains details on two of the gang members: the reference to Ferguson's Gang talks about Red Biddy's work in later life as a paediatrician who achieved notoriety when she 'kidnapped' a child who she felt was a risk from his parents; Sister Agatha's talent as a musician is mentioned and the fact that she worked for the Red Cross.

Using this information to scour old newspaper reports for child kidnapping cases from the 1970s it became clear that the kidnapping cited had involved a fourteen year old boy who Red Biddy sent off to Canada when his mother was institutionalised. The articles disclosed Red Biddy's real name was Rachel Pinney, a known Communist supporter, whose father was Major-General Pinney and whose uncle was the famous surgeon Sir Henry Head.

A general search on Red Cross stalwarts who had pursued a musical career elicited no results though; the identity of Sister Agatha remained a mystery.

The intimate relationship between the National Trust and Ferguson's Gang meant a smorgasbord of information regarding the Gang has been accumulated; in addition to the permanent exhibition at the Old Town Hall, Isle of Wight with the collage presented by Sister Agatha in 1989, there were also the archives at Heelis, Swindon. Here the original Boos were stored with the National Trust Annual Records, the Gang's embroidered robe and correspondence with the Gang over the past eighty years.

Buried within all of this information were vital clues which helped to unravel some of the outstanding mystery around Sister Agatha and Kate O'Brien; there were also some fascinating windows into Bill Sticker's life. Michael Maine, a young friend of Bill Stickers, recounted their friendship. Kitty Turnbull and Jean Gladstone, Bill Sticker's nieces, had been interviewed during which they had recalled Bill Stickers being born into a very grand

67

house with an army of servants; about the strained relationship between Bill and her mother when Bill would literally be sick with nerves at never appearing to meet her mother's expectations. Bill was obviously a force to be reckoned with though; Kitty and Jean's mother, Bill's sister-in-law, was very nervous of Bill Stickers initially; hardly surprising meeting such a vibrant personality. This was the opposite of their father who looked up adoringly to his brilliant older sister, however both parents found Bill's philanthropy trying in later life when, having given away all her worldly possessions, they were forced to look after her financially.

The correspondence provided the major breakthrough for Sister Agatha and Kate O'Brien The Nark's identities though. The first was a return letter to Sister Agatha which inadvertently used her real name (Mrs Jervis-Read), giving something concrete around which to start investigating Sister Agatha's true identity. Agatha had written to the Trust in 1966 to extend an invitation to the Gang's 40th Anniversary which was being planned on 27th May 1967 and the Gang was keen for the Trust to be able to attend.

The second was similar, an area agent in 1952 wrote to Miss O'Brien regarding the installation of a new toilet at the Gang's HQ. The 'Miss O'Brien' has to be 'Kate O'Brien The Nark' and there was a Hertfordshire address provided, finally there was something substantial with which to work on unmasking Kate's identity.

The final clue in the correspondence concerned Erb the Smasher; the documents relating to the BBC Broadcast show that the person who stood in for Ferguson during this appeal was Bill Sticker's brother, Robert Gladstone aka Erb the Smasher, because as Bill's glowing letter after listening to the appeal declares 'Superb Erb!'.

There was a flurry of letters with the British Broadcasting Corporation about the technical details of the appeal including the length of the script (advising to aim for 600 words). The address used for Erb was Messrs Wiggins, Teape & Alex Pirie. This company was a paper manufacturer with offices throughout Britain including Aldgate and Glasgow. Putting this with the hand written post-script on Erb's account of his drop-off being sent from the paper factory gives credence to the assumption that Erb was working for Wiggins, Teape & Alex Pirie at the time.

Reading through Merlin Waterson's book gives an insight into Erb's pseudonym. Rather than Erb's nickname being based on his violent tendencies, it was in fact because so many young ladies thought he was rather handsome – in fact some felt he was a total smasher!

Waterson also delved deeper into the relationship between Bill Stickers and Williams-Ellis; Bill had obviously become a close friend to both Clough and Amabel as her book 'Cornwall' which was illustrated by Sven Berlin was edited for Bill by this husband and wife team.

In 1963 Williams-Ellis celebrated his 80th birthday, Bill wrote an ode which accompanied the unveiling of a new piazza at Portmeirion when of course the baddie was Briaraeus the Octopus.

Having now the names, if not their life history, for three of the five inner-circle members, and three of their supporters (The Artichoke, Wife of the Artichoke and Erb the Smasher) it was crucial to establish who the final gang member was and whether Ferguson had actually existed.

As there were no immediate clues on either of these the first port of call was to the shops which were mentioned throughout the Boo and from the previous research to identify any account-holding customers who had ordered deliveries to Shalford Mill on the dates of the Gang's meetings. The Gang purchased their masks from Harrods, making a special trip to obtain them; however Harrods has no record of the purchase of these masks, and we do not know what masks were stocked by the store at the time.

Getting a blank with Harrods, the next shop was Fortnum & Mason, from whom the young ladies had food sent down to their meetings at Shalford Mill. The archivist at Fortnum & Mason was again not able to provide details of who had ordered the food on their account but was able to provide the entertaining menus which the Gang used. Looking at these it is possible to see that the menus were selected from 'Fortnum & Mason make *Entertaining* easy in your own home' and 'Entertaining made easy by Fortnum & Mason. Dainties entering Fortnum & Mason's two-by-two at 182 Piccadilly'.

Being no further forward in the search, a change of tact was required; instead a careful analysis of the backgrounds of the four known gang members, who they knew, where they had worked and anyone their family were friendly with was undertaken in the hope of uncovering the final two identities.

Starting with Sister Agatha it was possible to track back from her married name and establish that she had been christened Brynhild Granger. Agatha had an older sister, Isabelle, who went to Newnham; both girls were influenced by their artistic maternal grandfather, Thomas Dodd, and inherited the suffragette zeal of their paternal great aunt, Myra Sadd.

Continuing to delve into Sister Agatha's life meant starting with her school years. She went to school at Saint Felix in Lowestoft; the school is still there today and the Old Felicians society was able to confirm that Sister Agatha had been an alumnus of Saint Felix School. Looking back over the records though there was no listing for anyone from this time, so there were no classmates to try and follow up on.

There had been a suggestion that Agatha had attended the Royal Academy of Music, where her lover Harold Jervis-Read was a professor; however there was no student record for Agatha at the college to support this assumption, plus there is no time which isn't accounted for.

The next step was to look at the people she had lived with after leaving school to see if there was a flat-mate, however looking through the telephone directories of the time made no reference to any of the other residents.

A chance discovery of a series of letters written by Harold Jervis-Read to Sister Agatha provided an insight into her life from 1927 when she left school and about her joining the Royal Free Hospital as an Almoner. The letters were part of a set owned by Richard Ford Manuscripts; reading through them was fascinating; showing the tangled love-life, the ever-present fears and dreamy hopes of the pair. After leaving school Agatha attended King's College before moving across to the London School of Economics, living in halls of residence before sharing a flat at Airlie Gardens when she embarked on her training as an Almoner.

With still no name for Lord Beershop or Kate O'Brien the attention reverted back to Bill Stickers and Red Biddy to identify their social networks. Starting with Bill it became apparent that neighbours to the family home in Surrey included Ernest Shepherd at Shamley Green and the weekend homes of Clough Williams-Ellis and the Trevelyan family; their homes at Shere were rented from the Bray family, relations of the Godwin-Austens, also close neighbours. Williams-Ellis' inclusion of Bill Sticker's confession to being the founder of Ferguson's Gang suggests that he was not a member of the Gang at the time; on the other hand both Trevelyan and Godwin-Austen become instrumental supporters of the Gang during the latter years.

There was a chance that Bill Stickers may have recruited a Gang member from her school days; although bright and academic, her father sent her to Eversley School, Folkestone, which focused on being a strict more exclusive establishment, not something which appealed to the young Bill. The school was set up in 1905 by the younger sister of Charles Kingsley (author of the Water Babies) but had closed at the end of the last century. As the school was no longer functioning there was no point of contact to check the school records to see who Bill's classmates would have been. Instead the local library was able to provide two useful pieces of information. One was a background to the school which highlighted the good works the school actively encouraged (the girls sponsored a child's cot at Great Ormond Street Hospital); this training in charitable works obviously influenced the impressionable Bill and partly explains the zeal she attached to the work of the Gang.

The second piece of information regarded the Chaplain of Eversley School who also played a role in inspiring Bill. Unusually, this man of the cloth was an author and playwright who edited seven famous one-act plays, including his own entitled 'Campbell of Kilmohr', which was published by Penguin.

71

The most revealing fact about this Chaplain though was his name; he was called John Ferguson.

There is no evidence in Ferguson's papers to suggest he became actively involved in the Gang, instead it was his endearing spirit, love of theatrical suspense and championing of causes that gave Ferguson's Gang its name.

In 1922 Bill went up to Newnham College, Cambridge to study Oriental Languages and met Arthur Elton, later to become 10th Baronet, while he was studying English and Moral Sciences at Jesus. The pair were briefly affianced. Elton was mentioned in Althea Graham's diary, a student at Girton, the other female college of the time. She described Elton's passion for the movie business; he went on to become a film director and producer and afterwards became production head of Shell Petroleum Films. Unfortunately Althea's records fail to mention Elton's fiancée in any detail.

Originally it appeared that there were no firm friendships forged during the Cambridge years until re-reading the graduate books showed Bill's friendship with Prascovia Shoubersky, a Saint Felix alumnus who introduced Bill to Isabelle, Sister Agatha's sister, who also attended Newnham. Finally a tangible link was established between two of the Gang members. The friendship between Bill and Sister Agatha though was not instantaneous; in fact she had some hesitation in befriending her friend's sister.

Having established who Ferguson was and linked Bill to Sister Agatha the attention was turned to Red Biddy's friends. The majority of her papers, stored amongst her family records, post-dated the time of the Gang's most intense works; there were, however, diaries from the 1940s with names and addresses of friends which showed meetings organised with Sister Agatha and the dates her son, Peter, would come and stay. There was also personal correspondence with friends, many of them undated, including lovingly crafted letters from her husband Luigi.

The diaries showed that Red Biddy moved London residencies with an almost annual regularity, although she and Luigi did have a country house 'Beechlawn' in Hampshire which they also used. It is this address that was listed as Luigi's home when he formally changed his name from Cocuzzi to Cox and he took legal guardianship of his and Biddy's oldest son, an event which coincided with Red Biddy reverting to using her maiden name suggesting the start of the separation between the two. There was nothing to suggest who Kate O'Brien or Lord Beershop was though.

Focusing on Lord Beershop, examination of the Boo elicited a further clue; at the fourth meeting Lord Beershop extended an invite from her parents for the Gang to stay at the family's house en-route to Chester (for the Gang's visit to the Roman Amphitheatre). This suggests a location around the West Midlands or Shropshire area for the stop on the journey to be feasible. There was no exact mention of the place she lived, however it provided a reference point for confirming any future potential candidates.

The National Trust article had claimed that she had attended the Slade School of Art. This was supported by the 'Taming the Tentacles' exhibition which included several sketches by Lord Beershop; both believed she had been a student prize winner at the Slade.

In the first instance an analysis of the artwork of the Slade Alumni from the late 1920s to compare the style and composition with that of the drawing of Bill and Kate sewing curtains was undertaken. It showed that Helen Lessore (nee Brookes) had an almost identical style. However Helen lived at home while studying at the Slade, with no links to the Midlands. In addition there is no evidence from the correspondence or records that Sister Agatha had ever known Helen.

The next step was to trawl through the archives looking at the various records for prize winners' student records. By cross-referencing the students with Agatha the identity of Lord Beershop was discovered; she was Ruth Sherwood who resided at 8 Airlie Gardens, the same lodging address as Agatha.

Having identified a name and home address for Beershop it was then possible to establish her date of birth, her birthplace and who her family were. She was, in fact, related to both Rudyard Kipling and Prime Minister Stanley Baldwin.

Beershop had attended the Edgbaston Church of England College for Ladies; unfortunately once again this school closed when it was merged with Edgbaston College in 1999 to form St George's School. There is a memoir though written by a former headmistress, Mary Bowers, who talks about the history of the school and how every day the girls were forced to learn the verse of a new psalm. Perhaps this goes someway to explaining why Lord Beershop became so anti-religious in her attitudes.

While researching the family locally it transpired that an album of Lord Beershop's paintings had been donated by a distant relative. These had been compiled together with a brief history of each of the sitters and provided an illuminating insight into Beershop's local friends. Although none of the women appeared to be part of the inner-circle, there were potential candidates who may have been conscripted into joining the Gang.

The final member of the inner-circle still to be traced was Kate O'Brien The Nark. Within the Boo there were two pointers as to her home location; her report on 22nd January 1933 shows that she caught the 2.05pm from Paddington as she headed home. Then at the Gang's fifth meeting on 26th March 1933 Kate expressed a preference for investigating additional water mills for restoration in Shropshire.

By checking the train times for the 2.05pm trains leaving Paddington on 21st January 1933 it is possible to plot Kate's route home. However these two pieces of information proved to be contradictory. The destination for the train was a tube journey from Bishop's Road, Paddington stopping via Westbourne Park, Latimer Road and Kensington Addison Road; nowhere near the West Midlands or Shropshire, a seemingly frustrating dead-end.

Reverting attention back to the address included in correspondence from the 1950s it was possible to discover that the house owner of the time was Harry Gaze, later taken over by Philip Gaze. A search for Mr Gaze elicited that he was born in 1874 in Hartismore, Suffolk. He lived in London for most of his life and had been married twice. His second wife, Charlotte, was born in 1873 and had owned the Hertfordshire property at the time of Ferguson's Gang. It was possible that Charlotte was Kate O'Brien however she was distinctly older than the others, had

74

never attended King's College and came from a different era. There was no evidence of a connection with any of the other Gang members.

Harry and Charlotte did have one son, Philip. Investigating Philip's life it transpired that he was mentioned as the surviving spouse in The Times obituary in 1983. The newspaper article wrote about his wife, Mabel Gaze. It became apparent that it was Charlotte's daughter-in-law, Mabel, who was Kate O'Brien. By using her death dates and examining the marriage certificate it was established that Philip Gaze had married Mabel Joyce Maw in 1940 at the Radlett parish church, near to the original Hertfordshire address. Tracing Kate O'Brien's history back through her birth certificate it showed she was born in Shropshire but lived with an aunt in Kensington during the late 1920s. The discovery that her father had owned a famous encaustic tile business helped to trace the family history further. The local museum was able to confirm Kate had been educated at St Elphin's before attending King's College at the same time as Sister Agatha and Bill Stickers. The final inner-circle member of the Gang had eventually been revealed.

Chapter Seven: How the Gang united

The five individuals had now been unmasked: Bill Stickers was Margaret Gladstone, Sister Agatha was Brynhild Granger, Red Biddy was Rachel Pinney, Lord Beershop was Ruth Sherwood and Kate O'Brien was Mabel Maw. The question was how they had all come together; they lived in disparate parts of the UK with no obvious family connections between them.

A re-examination of their formative years showed that all of the Gang attended private boarding schools before going to university. Their educational years proved to be highly influential. For Bill Stickers the influence of the Chaplin John Ferguson was obviously intense, using his name and his theatrical approach to life for the Gang was a type of tribute to him.

Childhood friends can often become long-life friends as turned out to be the case with Sister Agatha and Red Biddy. It was already established that Sister Agatha had attended Saint Felix School; however the fortuitous discovery of a pencilled note starting 'Dear Daddy' was found within Red Biddy's papers. The half-legible scrawl asks her father to write to Matron asking Matron to allow Biddy to take part in games once again as her legs were improving. At the end by Red Biddy's signature was the name of her school – Saint Felix. Checking the records at Saint Felix it was possible to see that the girls were classmates.

Although Red Biddy and Sister Agatha were schoolroom friends they did not become acquainted with the other Gang members until university. Sister Agatha became introduced to Bill Stickers while Bill was at Cambridge University; the friendship deepened when Bill was enrolled on the Brides course (run for society debs) at King's College prior to her marriage in 1928. At the time Bill was living in Catherine Street, just down the road from the current site of King's College. Kate O'Brien had also enrolled at King's University at the same time as Sister Agatha and Bill Stickers and she lived in the same halls of residence as Sister Agatha initially.

Sister Agatha once again provided the link to Lord Beershop; although Lord Beershop was studying art at the Slade at the time she and Sister Agatha lodged at Airlie Gardens Sister

Agatha had left King's College and explains the time lapse of Beershop joining the Gang two years after their first meeting.

The final resounding proof that they met through King's College, if any further corroboration is required, was a letter from Sister Agatha to Harold Jervis-Read lamenting being the only one left to study at the college 'Ruth [Lord Beershop] has bought a hang-up meat safe today,' she wrote; 'No picnics here and no Rachel [Red Biddy] next door – I miss it! So Peggy [Bill Stickers] has given me a gramophone'.

So this was how the Gang were formed; five young society ladies from all over England, who were in London from 1927 to 1930, with a social conscience and a penchant for life. This meeting of souls was the catalyst for a lifelong dedication to their noble cause, despite the background of their tangled troubled personal stories.

England in the interwar period saw a state of flux never experienced before; the dedication that Ferguson's Gang showed in preserving England's heritage for us to enjoy and experience today is unprecedented yet they took the mantle of responsibility on with the same good spirit and joie-de-vivre as they showed over most of their lifetimes.

Then again, as one Gang member put it: 'We cared about helping to save England and wanted to be involved in something of permanent value. Together we decided to pool our wits into battle… we were in our early twenties and it was fun.'

Chapter Eight: Drafting Conscripted Members

Having unmasked the members of the inner-circle there were also clues uncovered about the Gang's subscribers which gave hints to the other individuals involved and where so much of the money came from.

The Gang's conscripted members included: Granny the Throttler, The Artichoke, Wife of the Artichoke, Poolcat, Erb the Smasher, Fred, Uncle Gregory, Black Maria, Silent O'Moyle, Pious Yudhishthira, Joshua Bottle-Washer, Jerry Boham, Sam, Sister Niphite, Is Nib, Outer Yam Yam and Mother Maudez.

Other supporters of the Gang included: Pore Old Harris, Samson, Anne of Lothbury, Sister Boadicea, Old Poll of Paddington, Matheson, Dulce, Forward Amanda and Volker Jake.

It has already been established that two of the Gang's subscribing members were the Artichoke and the Wife of the Artichoke; this pair became involved through the Gang's purchase of Shalford Mill. Although originally unknown to the Gang, the close working relationship over the next decade and the proximity of the Gang's HQ and the living quarters of the Artichoke's family meant the Artichoke and the Wife of the Artichoke were firmly ensconced in the Gang's circle of supporters. The Artichoke's mother, a strident suffragette, also became involved becoming known as 'Granny the Throttler' as an oblique reference to her work with new born babies.

Another supporter who has been unmasked was Erb the Smasher, Bill Sticker's brother; showing that he was involved in both delivering money and in making the BBC Broadcast on behalf of the Gang.

Erb's performance was congratulated by Bill Stickers; she wrote 'SUPERB ERB! I never erd a better speech. Never. Every word came out clear as a Bell and ow ever you got it so dramatic yr Slazenger alone knows. I couldn't av dun it 2 save me life.'

Someone within the Trust has noted (on a copy of the Radio Times) that the BBC broadcast raised over £900 during the following month and Princess Louise also personally wrote to the Gang on 29th August enclosing her donation and expressing sincere congratulations on the broadcast. The note about Erb's Slazenger is a sly poke at Erb's tennis fascination and it was no surprise a letter of felicitation in response to the BBC appeal also came from RMK Turnbull, the Wimbledon Tennis Champion. Turnbull was a close compatriot of both Erb and his wife Naomi, who was also a Wimbledon player, and she may well have been dubbed 'Fred' by the Gang after Fred Perry, the upcoming tennis star of the time.

Erb and Fred were not the only members of Bill Sticker's family to be involved. Great Uncle Gregory, who was due to deliver money but in the end was away in America, first appeared in Bill Sticker's life while she was at Cambridge and eventually went on to become her husband.

The Boo provided additional clues to two of the other subscribers as well. At the fourth meeting on 10th December 1932, Lord Beershop extended an invitation from her advisers to the Gang, 'The Advisers' are in fact Lord Beershop's parents who lived at Sutton Coldfield.

There had been previous suggestions that Black Maria was another name for the Wife of the Artichoke, their signatures look very similar occasionally. However the true identity of Black Maria, which is revealed in a number of ways, appears to challenge this supposition. In the ninth meeting on 16th March 1934, the Gang report that Black Maria's chauffeur collected the Gang from Ryde and drove them to the Old Court House at Newtown. This suggests that Black Maria was a local, living on or near the Isle of Wight and it is her house that the Gang go to later in the day.

Although it is clear that Black Maria had a home on the Isle of Wight she also had houses elsewhere. The evening of the National Trust dinner mentioned how the Gang met up at Black Maria's hole, a central London apartment or house, which gave easy access to The Dorchester Hotel for the group. Black Maria at this time had sold the house at Cadogan Square and had a London residence in Westminster.

At the meeting between Mr Colenutt and the Artichoke, when the question over the cost of renovation arose, Black Maria unhesitatingly guaranteed the money. She was obviously a woman of extreme wealth who had control over her own finances.

The final clue came from the drop of money made by Silent O'Moyle who dropped off the money accompanied by a 'bottle of poison' (home-made sloe gin) brewed by Black Maria and Bill Stickers.

Taking all this information into account and comparing it to the information known about Bill Stickers, the most obvious candidate for Black Maria was Bill Sticker's mother, Mrs John Gladstone.

With Lord Beershop's and Bill Sticker's families roped into the Gang's activities, it is unsurprising that Silent O'Moyle turned out to be another parent of a Gang member. There are a number of references to Silent O'Moyle within the Boo. The first is when Kate O'Brien required masks for her drop; her father accompanied her to buy them at Harrods. The second is when Silent O'Moyle made the secret delivery of money. The third is the arrival of Kate O'Brien and Silent O'Moyle together at Black Maria's on the night of the dinner at The Dorchester. The similarity between the surnames 'O'Brien' and 'O'Moyle' supports the theory that Silent O'Moyle was in fact Kate O'Brien's father.

Sister Agatha was very close to her own sister, Isabelle; they shared the same emancipated pioneering spirit. Between Sister Agatha and Bill Stickers they conscripted her as Sister Niphite.

Apart from family connections, there were close friends involved as well; the Boo holds an intriguing document – a 'letter patient' which gave Bill Stickers the power to act as Ferguson's deputy at the Gang's formal opening of the HQ; it was signed by Jerry Boham and Josh B Washer. Later on there is a note from Josh using his full name (Joshua Bottle-Washer) who made reference to Jerry and another member, Sam. The interesting point around the second note was the paper it had been written on; Joshua reused a sample page from a Birmingham paper factory, Kalamazoo. These three turned out to be close friends of Lord Beershop's from the Midlands.

Family friends were also embroiled; just as the Second World War broke out Bill Stickers wrote to Matheson regarding the Newtown project. The note starts with a slight rejoinder about the cost of the renovation and goes on to say that the Gang would not stand in the way of the Trust in relation to the Hall's use (obviously disregarding the heated discussions recorded in the Boo). The National Trust archives show Bill wrote 'If Poolcat can't make it pay, then give to old man Colenutt and let him fill it with fossils and see if that is a bigger draw'.

The reference here is obvious; the Gang's preference to have the building used by the YHA is finally deemed unworkable by the Trust, so it is to be used as a museum. The reference to 'Poolcat' was recognisable; he was an ardent supporter of the Youth Hostelling movement, an active member of the National Trust committee and Bill Sticker's childhood neighbour, GM Trevelyan.

There were two further Gang members conscripted, although no mention of their designated pseudonyms were given. In Bill Sticker's personal correspondence a series of letters spanning a large part of her life were exchanged with CS Lewis (author of the Narnia tales). His interest in two of the sites prompted the Gang to make donations. His friend, AP Herbert, also became involved. The second Boo contained an episode of discovery which he undertook with the Gang.

The final members of the circle who are known were much later additions from the end of the last century. Correspondence held by the National Trust shows they had been back in touch with Bill and invited her along to a party; Bill thanks the editor of the National Trust magazine for the note ('Then-Q 4 your card') and then asks if the editor is the same person 'as went 2 the north pole... she was a dutch doll and saved them all from being eat up by an eagle'. The name stuck and the editor, Sarah-Jane Forder, was henceforth known as 'Dutch Doll'.

The last recruit of the Gang was found in the National Trust exhibition talking about his friendship with Bill Stickers. He again appeared in Claire Riche's book; she described how Michael Maine had been involved in raising money to save the

81

lost shrine of Liskeard. It appears Bill had bestowed upon him the title of 'Pegasus'.

This journey of discovery turned up a number of surprises in pursuit of uncovering the five maidens behind the masks. The head of the gang had been identified, the inner circle of the five key members have been revealed for the first time since the Gang were formed, along with sixteen of their conscripted supporters and two known literary giants.

What also became apparent during this journey was just how well connected the girls were; their social circles meant they were regularly mixing with the celebrities of the twenties and thirties. They moved in the highest cliques of the political, literary and musical elite. Yet this cosseted lifestyle only stifled them; each felt the need for a more liberated way of life. The personal stories behind the pseudonyms showed that each had their own private tragedies to contend with throughout their lives, making their dedication to the cause of preserving England even more remarkable. These stories are told here.

Part 3: Unmasking the Gang

Chapter Nine: The Inner-Circle Gang Members

The social turbulence experienced by the girls as they grew up has already been illustrated; their family fortunes and way of life were changing for ever, fuelled by the Great Depression after the Wall Street crash in October 1929 and unemployment rising to almost 3 million in 1932.

Yet against this backdrop there was an explosion of creativity for the population to enjoy en-mass, rather than being segregated by class as previously. In 1935 Penguin Books published their first sixpence books; the ten titles included works by Ernest Hemingway and Agatha Christie and sold three million copies that year. The British Broadcasting Corporation was awarded its Royal Charter in 1927 so that it could 'inform, educate and entertain'; and the first 'talkie' film – The Jazz Singer – was shown in 1928. It was something the Gang members embraced wholeheartedly.

This blast from the arts (whether literary, paintings, music or design) was having a profound effect; no longer was society tied to its traditions of yester-year. The rise of groups such as the Bloomsbury Set saw people reacting against 'the bourgeois habits... the conventions of Victorian life'. The likes of Virginia Woolf, also an alumni of King's College, John Maynard Keynes and EM Forster spellbound the world with their avant-garde outputs and laissez-faire approach to personal relationships; something which Ferguson's Gang, probably unconsciously, came to emulate.

There was also the rise of the Arts and Crafts movement and the romantic interpretation of the Gothic era which reverted back to using traditional crafts, often with simple forms from medieval, romantic or folk styles of decoration. This philosophy spilt over from their work into their personal beliefs for embedding it within society; Thomas Hardy and William Morris were strong advocates of SPAB, Beatrix Potter was an outspoken supporter of the National Trust and Sir Patrick Abercrombie founded CPRE. The Gang's acceptance of this was obvious, they sought out traditional craftsmen when looking at furniture and their robe was embroidered with 'Art polishes and improves nature', a sentiment totally in line with that of William Morris.

The Gang, however, were modern idealists who balanced this juxtaposition of retaining heritage with their own feminist beliefs. They were political, astute and well-connected; empowered through emancipation. They saw women such as Viscountess Astor, the MP for Plymouth and owner of Cliveden, Berkshire, playing an active role in the National Trust. However their own personal troubled lives made them dependent upon the Gang. Each member has their own unique story

John Ferguson

John Alexander Ferguson, the inspiration behind Ferguson's Gang, was born 1871 at Callander, Perthshire; although he wrote under Ferguson he was also known as Frederick Watson. He was a Scottish clergyman, playwright and mystery writer. He was brought up by his grandmother, Mrs Thomas Ferguson, who looked after Ferguson and his three brothers and one sister. After leaving school he was employed as a railway clerk at Callander before he finally decided to become ordained.

At 19, while still living at Callander's station buildings, he enrolled as an Episcopalian Chaplain; part of the world-wide Anglican Communion. His ministry then took him to Dundee, Guernsey, Glasgow and Drumtotchy before he became Chaplain at Eversley School, Folkestone and entered into Bill Stickers' life.

He was Chaplain at the school from 1915 to 1938, living out of school at Devonshire Terrace, Sandgate. He may well have chosen this location because of the literary-rich environment; his neighbours included the writers: HG Wells, who built Spade House there, fellow Scot, Sir James Barrie, GK Chesterton and Bernard Shaw.

Most of Ferguson's literary output was during his time as Chaplain, He wrote ten books from 1918 to 1943 including *The Man in the Dark* published in 1928. The summary of this book from the 1952 Penguin edition was: 'Murder on a foggy night at Ealing in the presence of a down-and-out who couldn't see the crime; a long car drive taking two people to hide for a while in the country; pursuit by journalists; a blind man's love affair; the criminal's escape finally and dramatically prevented. These are the ingredients of a part-mystery, part-adventure story which describes with equal brilliance and from both angles the problems of the hounds and the dodges of the hares.' Critics acclaimed these works, one saying 'As no two of his stories are in any sense repetitious, it is probably his practice of setting each tale against the background in which he writes that gives this variety in characterization and action to each of his works.' He held international acclaim with his books published into nine foreign languages.

He was also a playwright; his one act play *The Scarecrow* was first produced by the Dramatic Company of the Arts League of Service on 21st October 1921 at Maidstone. This was the first truly mobile theatre group, made possible by the use of Countess de la Warr's Daimler station-wagonette. Ferguson also wrote *The King of Morven* (1922) and *Claire de Lune* (1936) dedicated to Nona Johnston; however his most famous play was *Campbell of Kilmohr*. At the Royalty Theatre production the Glasgow Herald dramatic critic hailed it as a 'new and significant type of drama'.

Ferguson went on to be editor for several books of one act plays, published by Penguin. In one of these *Seven famous one act plays*, his fellow contributors included Clifford Box, Oliphant Down, Stanley Houghton and AP Herbert. It may well be through this life-long association between Ferguson and Herbert that Herbert went on to be introduced into Ferguson's Gang and conscripted in as an honorary member.

Ferguson left Eversley School in 1939 when he moved to take up the ministry at Culross where he lived at Duimarle Castle; a castle overlooking the Forth only 16 miles from Edinburgh which had fine grounds and was of historic interest. It was here that Macbeth's wife and child were murdered by Macbeth. While not quite so extreme, Ferguson almost lost his life here as well. In a bizarre accident his French stone water-bottle was heating up as usual one evening when it suddenly exploded like a bomb, smashing the grate, bringing down a blast of soot and covering everything in acid, destroying furniture and furnishings. The acid spray also burnt Ferguson's hands and face but luckily his eyes remained unharmed.

He retired in 1946, when his wife died, and moved back to the house he owned in Lymington, Hampshire. It had been rented out to an Irish Colonel who had not kept the house in good order. Ferguson had purchased the house and grounds when MGM had bought the silent rights to *Night in Glengyle*. The house was near to the Pier Station and had views out across the Solent to Yarmouth, giving Bill an additional incentive to save the Old Town Hall at Newtown. Returning to the south coast, which held so many fond memories for him, gave him a solace in his final years. He died on 3rd December 1952 leaving all of his estate to the Fund of the Episcopal Church of Scotland.

His correspondence shows no mention of being involved with Ferguson's Gang nor does his location tally with any of the sites they saved. He did however have an immense influence on the highly impressionable Bill Stickers; bequeathing to her his love of theatrical dramatics.

Bill Stickers (will be prosecuted)

The Early Years

Bill Stickers was born as Margaret Steuart Gladstone on 1st March 1904; at this time the family were living at 2 Whitehall Court, London. Her father was John Steuart Gladstone, nephew of William Ewart Gladstone, the former Prime Minister. Like many of the Gladstone family, John worked as an East India Merchant and this lucrative trade funded Bill's privileged upbringing. Although the East India Company had been wound up some thirty years before, the family were still continuing to trade with India. His uncle Robertson Gladstone had established offices in Liverpool, Calcutta and London. The family business also stretched west, dealing in corn in the US, cotton from Brazil as well as having extensive plantations in the West Indies, similar to Red Biddy's family.

John had been born and raised in the North, however by the time of his marriage to Margaret he had moved to London; then when Bill was seven and Robert, her younger brother, was four the family moved to Nanhurst at Cranleigh, a house on the Bray Estate. It was here that Bill's family met the Godwin-Austens, Trevelyans and the teenage CS Lewis, who was studying in a neighbouring village.

Other weekend neighbours, who the family socialised with, included Clough and Amabel Williams-Ellis, EH Shepherd, illustrator of the Winnie-the-Pooh stories, the politician St John Broderick, 1st Earl of Midleton, Conservative MP and Thomas Cecil, 1st Baron Fairer of Abinger, County Councillor and a member of the Surrey Archaeological Society. This eclectic mix gave the young Bill Stickers a rare insight into the political and creative thinking of the day.

Bill was baptised at the family church, Westminster, the place she would also later marry at. Her Anglican upbringing never appears to have dominated her life, indeed for years she flirted with alternative deities and religions from paganistic rituals, interests in cosmic worship and a study of Hinduism. In her later life, like her contemporary Penelope Betjeman, she became a devout Roman Catholic, dedicating her time to helping others less fortunate.

While living at Nanhurst she invented a 'holy tree'; worshiping a tree within the 79 acre garden as though it was a high God, even encouraging her brother to participate in the rituals. When she began attending boarding school it was no wonder that the influence of a charismatic and unusually vibrant Chaplain made such a lasting impression on Bill.

Bill excelled at school work, being a natural scholar. There is little now on record about the school, what we know comes from GP Warner, the warden of the college in 1973. 'The building of Eversley College, lying back in its own grounds from Coolinge Lane in Folkestone, was first erected in 1905-1906 and formed a purpose-built Girls' School, of the stricter and more exclusive type. The school had rather a brief life. It flourished until the thirties but that difficult decade and the looming shadow of war brought its career to an end though some of its pupils transferred to a sister college at Leamington.'

The Folkestone Gazette's report from 1967 celebrated 'The old days of Eversley'. 'In 1910 it was established at the existing stately-looking building... In its earliest days the school published each term The Eversley Papers. One of these mentions that 'just before the end of term Miss White gave a fancy dress dance to which she invited the girls and two or three others.' Observe that those of the outside world, even then, were apparently not welcome.'

At the turn of the 1920s young ladies' fashions made a radical shift; gone were the formal tight-waisted skirts and full-sleeved blouses with high necks and in came the more fluid look of the flapper. This daring attire not only made a statement about women's rights to wear what they wanted but it also gave them far greater physical freedom than had ever been available before. It was a fashion that Bill embraced whole heartedly, much to the horror of her father.

The relationship between Bill and The Da and Mammie was complex; although she adored her father he, as a traditionalist, found it difficult to understand his clever intelligent daughter. In an era when women were expected to secure a successful marriage, options such as tertiary education were still foreign concepts. Like many fathers John Gladstone believed no man wanted a highly educated wife. The relationship between Bill and her mother was far more complicated. Margaret Gladstone was a bright woman who had successfully married into a prominent British family; however she felt thwarted by the lack of opportunities available to women in her generation. She pushed Bill to be the epitome of a successful woman, championing her daughter's right to university education, the ability to move in the highest social circles and to catch a highly eligible husband. This intensity caused an underlying friction in the mother-daughter relationship. Bill would often suffer from migraines and other psychosomatic illnesses as a result of Margaret's expectations; Bill constantly worried about not living up to her mother's hopes.

The Salad Years

Margaret's insistence on Bill continuing her education must have borne some weight with her husband as Bill applied and was accepted to go down to Cambridge to study Oriental Languages. Self-teaching herself before she went demonstrated her ability to apply herself wholeheartedly to achieving a task. Unfortunately her father died six months before the term started at Cambridge, so he never witnessed the illustrious academic success Bill made at university.

There were only two options at Cambridge for women in those days, Girton or Newnham; Bill joined alongside a number of other students including Enid Mary Russell-Smith and Prascovia Shoubersky both of whom had attended Saint Felix School. It is through the Saint Felix connection that these two introduced Bill to one of the new girls in 1924, Isabelle Granger, who was also studying at Newnham.

The vistas offered by university life provided a freedom that Bill had never experienced before; she threw herself into student life. As a natural scholar Bill took the rigorous academic demands in her stride, leaving plenty of time for the social aspects of university life. There were the usual Cambridge forays; hockey against Girton, Reruse and Ely; visiting Steffers the bookshop, watching the 'The Epic of Everest' in the Guildhall and afternoon tea at Bonds.

Bill continued with her art using her talent to hoodwink fellow students into believing she owned several masterpieces. Her artistic abilities were recognised in a more formal way in later years when she was invited to exhibit her watercolours at the Paris Salon in 1955 and 1956.

Nobody was spared her sharp wit, she bestowed nicknames on everyone; even her Aunt Cecil's relation, Viscount Chetwynd was included. It was obviously the start of Bill's thought process in devising the use of pseudonyms for Ferguson's Gang.

The sweeping changes affecting society swept through Newnham College as well. Skirts were shortened to reveal ankles and calves for the first time and Bill even took the drastic step of having her hair cut short. Like their Bloomsbury set predecessors there was a flirtation with the idea of laissez-faire relationships and tentative explorations into the concept of lesbianism for many. Bill adopted her father's speech, using the northern colloquialisms he picked up in his boyhood; she often referred to ladies as 'Judies', a term meaning girl-friend.

Within Bill's circle were Prascovia Shoubersky, Sheelah Stoney-Archer and Enid Mary Russell-Smith; Prascovia went on to become Mrs Tchitchkyn and Sheelah worked as an Assistant at Harrods, at a time when the Gang were frequenting it to purchase their masks, before marrying and becoming Mrs Clutton-Brock although soon afterwards she died aged only 34.

In 1925 Bill graduated with a First Class Honours degree, becoming the first woman to gain this in the Oriental Languages Tripos Part I (Sanskrit) and Part II (Pali); the award provoked much mirth from the male students. Although female students were allowed to study and take exams they did not receive the same recognition as male students at Cambridge, although they secured the title - the much-joked-about BA tit – they did not have the substance of degrees. After completing her first degree she went on to be awarded the Caroline Turle Scholarship and remained another year at Newnham to do the first year's research for her MA. She finally left Newnham in 1926.

Upon her father's death the family home moved away from Surrey to the Isle of Wight. Bill lived here during the holidays while she was at Cambridge and on-and-off during the period before her marriage. Although no records exist of Bill attending King's College to continue her studies, the Evening News was adamant that the Gang had met at college. It is most likely that her mother enrolled Bill onto the Brides course at King's College which apparently imparted its own special flavour to the college atmosphere.

At this time Bill had her own digs at Catherine Street, just across from the current King's College campus; she was waiting for her fiancé, Uncle Gregory, to complete his degree and join her in London. The relationship between the two was unusual but Gregory's undemanding presence may have provided an attractive escape route from the intense relationship Bill had with her mother. One thing was clear for both parties, neither contemplated having children. Contraception and birth control were coming to the forefront of the women's agenda with Marie Stopes' revolutionary family planning clinics and oral contraception becoming available. Interestingly Marie Stopes was a mutual friend of both Ferguson (through Noel Coward) and Red Biddy (through Thomas Hardy). For Bill and Gregory they felt strong enough about the subject to arrange the omission of any reference to child bearing from their wedding ceremony.

As part of the marriage, a settlement was made by the Gladstone family on the couple; on 29th June 1928 Robert Gladstone, in the presence of two lawyers, made a settlement in consideration of the marriage of £10,000 war stock, £7,000 Mersey Docks bonds and £2,022 LMS Railway stock. In today's values this equates to a dowry of just under a million pounds.

The wedding took place two days later at St Margaret's, Westminster, the church situated in the grounds of Westminster Abbey on Parliament Square. There was minimum fuss and little of the pomp and circumstance which usually accompanied a society wedding of the time; instead the marriage was witnessed by Uncle Gregory's father, Bill's mother and Christopher Bailey. It was completed in a record nine and half minutes, the curate remembering to omit the references to children. Perhaps this

94

omission was prophetic, in the end the marriage was never consummated and Bill was forced to look outside of her marriage for sexual fulfilment.

One such attachment was with an unnamed lady; perhaps Bill was unconsciously harking back to the close compatriotic warmth of her salad days. In a letter to Sister Agatha Bill wrote: 'Deare the ladey as give me up i think. This was the sonick i sent er:

Enough! I will not hazard anymore;
I take you up the gage of Britomart,
But tranquil to the spectre world depart
Which was my sanctuary long before,

To kissing reeds upon a misty shore
Where his Diphad with uneering dark
Strikes down Antares of the Scorpion Heart
And I the valiant Betelgeuse adore

In skyline-mist I vanish from your sight
And you shall never break my dream again
Or blind my eyes with unrelenting light,

Nor love, nor any Passion known to men
Shall guide pursuing feet into the night.
Goddess, I choose the way of Origen.'

She adds with a slight waspishness towards her blighted lover 'I don't need 2 explane the allusions 2 yew need i. I ad 2 supply footnots [to her]'.

Cornwall
Immediately after their marriage Bill moved into Uncle Gregory's bachelor digs at Dean's Yard, Westminster from where Gregory worked as a journalist and Bill lived as a society wife. However within a year they had upped sticks and moved to St Mawes, Cornwall. Perhaps strangely, given their privileged backgrounds and healthy marriage endowment, they chose not to

live in one of the grand houses on St Anthony's Headland; instead they resided in a terraced fisherman's cottage with Bill living in the two rooms downstairs and Gregory in the two rooms above where they could hear each other laughing as they avidly read. It was certainly a curious arrangement but one which seemed to give both parties the freedom they needed and the companionship they required.

The move to Cornwall started Bill's second greatest passion after Ferguson's Gang. The county had obvious attractions to both Bill and Gregory; for Gregory it gave him the proximity to the sea where he could totally indulge his passion for sailing. For Bill Cornwall held fond memories of holidays with Sister Agatha where the two young ladies would catch the train down from Paddington to St Ives and stay at the grand hotel Tregenna Castle, just up the hill from the local station. The hotel had been purpose-built by the Great Western Railway Company to cater for the increasing numbers of holiday makers who were visiting aboard their trains. The rooms offered magnificent views over the bay and a rare quality of light for Bill's sketching. Here the two of them would indulge themselves with traditional Cornish cream teas and junkets.

Cornwall during the interwar years was still a rural idyll, remote and distant from London and its society circles. Here fashions were slower to permeate, local dialects prevailed and the pace of life was still attuned to a more feudal England. These features would certainly have appealed to Bill's aesthetic sensitivities towards preserving this quintessential Englishness. She tried to capture some of the more endearing scenes she came across in day-to-day life within her book *Cornwall*, which was illustrated by Sven Berlin and edited by the Williams-Ellis'. The book was published by Paul Elek Publishers and the vignettes of rural life are memory-evoking.

'Not far from St. Mawes lived a simple soul who took it into his head to go a railway journey for the first time in his life. He entered the booking office, and approaching the tickethole asked for a return ticket. "Where to?" asked the Clerk. "Back 'ere," was the reply. The clerk, perceiving that this might be a troublesome case, asked him to wait a bit... The woman in front

96

of him asked for a return ticket and clerk asked "Where to?" "Mary Tavy," said the woman. This made it clear enough and when the worthy man was once again asked "Where to?" he simply replied "Charlie Emmett".' This charming recollection was also included in a letter from Bill to Erb to show how different life for her now was.

Bill's move away from London to a remote rural area showed great similarities with one of the National Trust's other female benefactors of the time – Beatrix Potter. Both Bill and Potter came from wealthy families, had young engagements which were broken off (although in the case of Potter this was through the untimely death of her betrothed) and were fervent supporters of the traditional agricultural-based way of life. Both women were published writers and accomplished artists, both left London for a more secluded retreat where they were free to run their own households and estates (Bill to Cornwall and Potter to the Lake District) and by doing so both learnt a new set of farming skills. Potter went on to manage the 2,000 acres of farmland and woodland she owned and became a leading figure in the Herdwick sheep breeders circle.

Similarly Bill adopted a hands-on-approach; joining the Cornwall branch of the Women's Land Army Committee in 1939 for the war effort and learning about the husbandry and breeding of goats, something for which she became well-known for locally. This resulted in her setting up a goat farm in Quenchwell, which features in her book *Cornwall*; the goats have a whole chapter dedicated to them with the tongue in cheek title 'Goats in heaven'.

'Hard by the well is a distinguished herd of pedigree dairy goats. In spring the canopy of the well is likely to be a leaping mass of kids. The goats are not purely decorative; they supply the congregation of Quenchwell Chapel, which is a highly remarkable body.' Bill mentions several of her goats by name: Satya Raka named after the Vedic goddess of the full moon, Ardoch Aneta, Rajalida (Delight of Kings) and Floyds Floxey, a giant Anglo-Nubian. Space began to become a premium at the goat farm and required more land; on 14th December 1945, Bill registered the land at 91 Pydar Street, Truro as part of her goat empire – Satya Goat Farm, Quenchwell Feeck.

Bill was also active in the CPRE which sought to save several holy sites at the time; she became Honorary Secretary from April 1936 to 1946 for the Cornwall branch, taking over from Arthur Treve Holman. She found a kindred spirit in the branch's Chairman, John Charles Williams, Lord Lieutenant for Cornwall. As well as a mutual friend of the Trevelyan family, he introduced Bill to the Rt Rev J W Hunkin, Bishop of Truro and also championed the National Trust. He donated 108 acres at Nare Head in 1931 to them and supported Bill's efforts to save large tracts of Cornish coastline. Having Williams' support meant Bill was able to be instrumental in lobbying Cornish coast landowners to sell, donate or covenant tracts of land to the National Trust, saving them from being blighted by bungalows. It was during this time she wrote the Mayon Castle poem *Bricks and a load of concrete* and *For they be a-building in Wide- mouth Bay, With their bungalows, garages, cinemas, restaurants, tea-houses, caravans, Jerry-built villas and all*. Her work at CPRE was paid tribute to in the 1935 and 1936 National Trust Annual Reports and she was included as the local contact within the 1938 Annual Report.

During this time she produced a campaign poem which was used by Williams-Ellis entitled: 'The Ballard of the Bypass'. The only known copy of the poem is held in the CPRE archives.

The jerrybuilder lay dreaming
In his golden fourpost bed;
He dreamt of an endless ribbon
Of bungalows pink and red
With fancy work on the gables
To every purchaser's choice:
And he dreamt in the back of his conscience
He heard old England's voice:-

"Don't build on the By-Pass, Brother:
Give ear to our last appeal!
Don't advertise where it tries the eyes

And distracts the man at the wheel.
You've peppered the landscape, Brother,
And blotted out half the sky:
Get further back with your loathsome shack,
Let the By-Pass pass you by!"

In addition to the work she did with the Gang to save properties, Bill also made separate donations. In 1936 The Times announced the appeal to save Rodborough Common, near Stroud, Gloucestershire. The sum required was £700, of which £250 had already been raised locally. Bill Stickers donated £3 to the cause and the National Trust managed to raise a total of £713 0s 5d. The appeal added over 250 acres on the top of the Cotswolds and preserved the natural beauty of the common.

Actively supporting these activities did not stop Bill from becoming involved with other disparate communities in Cornwall; her natural fluency with language remained. Bill, like Red Biddy became fluent in Russian; during the war she used her translation skills to help Russian sailors being nursed and cared for at Trelissick Hospital to keep in touch with their families and loved ones. Routinely her tall striding figure would be seen entering the cottage hospital to take down letters from the injured before typing them up on her trusted old typewriter (the very same one she used to type up her love poem for her fickle lover).

She continued studying languages, completing her PhD in 1952, almost three decades after starting and published numerous articles on Sanskrit and Eastern Christian texts. In true socialist style Bill used her languages to help others learn; in 1956 she became a teacher at the Probus School, Truro before going onto the St Austell Technical Institute to teach Russian for three years.

Living in Cornwall bewitched Bill, away from the formalities of society she was able to flourish, living life according to the Bloomsbury Set's creed of informal attitudes and individualism. As well as continuing her active leadership of Ferguson's Gang, her work at the CPRE and the Land Army, Bill blossomed in her own self-belief. She took to wearing comfortable, if unconventional, outfits and a patterned scarf around her head in Eastern European style.

She was interested in preserving the Cornish language and her mutual friend, through CS Lewis, Alfred Kenneth Hamilton Jenkin introduced her to becoming a Cornish Bard. He had been a founder bard of the Gorseth Kernow in 1928, taking the name Lef Stenoryon (Voice of the Tinners). A decade later Pollard followed in his footsteps to become a Cornish-language bard. As a member of the Cornish Gorsedd Bill and Jenkin were part of the group who gathered to celebrate the culture of Cornwall and act as protectors of its linguistic and cultural traditions. Bill took the name Arlodhes Ywerdhon 'Irish Lady', after the rock at the north end of Gamper Bay, near Land's End - part of the estate of Mayon Cliff Ferguson's Gang purchased in 1935. The rock's eponym comes from a marooned woman who was unable to be rescued. As well as her bardic involvement Bill also learnt to play the Irish harp, becoming a Gorseth harpist from 1948 to 1953 which meant she used a harp built in 1830 for the ritual ceremonies.

Bill's poetic outpourings have been mentioned, the love letter, the ditty to the National Trust and the ode to Williams-Ellis for his birthday celebrations; as has her book *Cornwall*. However the involvement with the Gorseth provided fresh inspiration and recalling the work produced by Ferguson while at Eversley, Bill wrote a number of 'mystery plays'. As ever these were sharp, insightful and witty; Synt Avaldor gained the Gorseth prize in 1941 while Synt Tanbellen was a parody of the Gorseth members; sadly none of the original scripts survive today.

Bill had been awarded the Gorseth prize the year before for her *Bewnans Alysaryn*, 'The life of Alysaryn' which was published in 1941. This work once again managed to be both satirical and serious; the play includes the Saint's life performed over two days which is broken down into eleven short days. Making a play on the medieval texts she provided stage directions in spoof early English (not unlike the mockney she often used in correspondence) so that one character 'goeth completelie dottie' and in another instance the stage recommendations for the end of the second day are that, 'if expense bee no object, let them set fire to the house for a spectacular curtaine'.

The play though had a more moralistic undertone. The hero, Alysaryn, was a rather modern day saint, worker and martyr who found himself caught between God and a close encounter with Beelzebub. However Alysaryn remained stalwartly true to himself and his beliefs, culminating in the play ending with several hymns. This religious ending coincided with the start of Bill's theological journey to return to her Christian origins.

Later Life

As the Gang grew older the difficulty in meeting up increased as commitments around families and work took up their time. No longer were they able to save the prodigious numbers of properties for the National Trust that they had been able to do previously.

Before Bill became a teacher she worked for the Rt Rev Joseph Hunkin, OBE, MC, DD when he was the eighth Bishop of Truro. Like Ferguson he was a charismatic man whose published work included *Is it Reasonable to Believe?* in 1935. He and Bill shared a strong evangelical streak and burgeoning social conscience; Hunkin used a shepherd's crook of iron as his pastoral staff; on the wooden shaft of which was a silver band inscribed 'Un para, un bugel' which is Cornish for 'One flock, one shepherd'. There was a mutual strong respect between Bill and Hunkin; Bill dedicated *Cornwall* to Hunkin with 'affectionate admiration'.

The exposure to Hunkin's zeal completed Bill's conversion. In the 1950s she became a staunch Roman Catholic, taking up the Catholic cause with the same fanaticism as she had with Ferguson's Gang, raising funds and supporting good works.

In 1973 the new church for Truro opened and once again Bill played a primary role in achieving this. The church had a joint dedication to Our Lady of the Portal & St Piran. Both of these are significant; the reference to Our Lady of the Portal reflected the discovery that, in mediaeval times, there was a Guild of Our Lady of the Portal whose duty was to maintain the bridge

101

over the river; St Piran, the other benefactor, was an early Saint of Cornwall and the Saint of tin miners.

A tapestry by Bill hangs in the Baptistery which shows the Coronation of Our Lady, surrounded by a group of Saints (the Fourteen Holy Helpers). This is copied from a shrine in Vierzehnheiligen in Bavaria, the spot where Bill's ashes were taken to as her final resting place.

Bill's embroidery talents were well documented in the Gang's ceremonial robe, which she helped to design and sew, and something which she continued to do throughout her life. Her piece-de-resistance though was the tapestry she designed and embroidered depicting the scenes from the Narnia Chronicles in 1983. It was a work of love and homage to her friend CS Lewis, glorifying his books. The tapestry measured 1,338 feet long and was entered into the Guinness Book of Records as one of the longest tapestry works ever (longer than the Bayeux Tapestry which is 230 feet long) and gained Bill publicity on both Radio Cornwall and Blue Peter.

Bill continued to be involved with the Guild of our Lady of the Portal from the 1960s to her death, continuing the air of mystery she created in Ferguson Gang. Each member of the Guild was known by a number only; Bill was Sister 10 or X. Together members said the rosary in pairs by telephone each evening and it was said that in the late 1970s the local exchanges were jammed by the Hail Marys being recited at the given hour.

During this time her faith must have provided her a valuable support; the 1960s was a time of grief and despair. Her mother, who had moved away from the family home on the Isle of Wight, joined her daughter in Cornwall to live as a recluse for the remainder of her life. Because of their complex relationship this gave Bill incredibly mixed feelings; having worked so hard for independence from the matriarchal dominance she was now forced to give it up to care for Margaret.

Her mother died in 1962, just six years later Uncle Gregory died leaving Bill a widow for the next 30 years. However with her stalwart determination she continued to throw herself into charitable works. While in her seventies Bill continued to use her Russian language to translate akathist hymns from the Church Slavonic, even managing to find one for Our Lady of the Portal, and these were printed by the Society of St John Chrysostom. Once again Bill put her own indomitable mark on them, making them witty and catchy to sing whether in Latin, Cornish or English.

She began to lose her sight but still her good works continued. She gave away all her worldly goods to charity and went on collecting for African nuns and organised a pilgrimage to Vierzehnheiligen in Germany for her 80th birthday.

One of the last causes Bill became passionately involved in was saving the shrine of Our Lady at Ladye Park in Liskeard. The remains of the shrine were discovered by Bill in 1955 after a remarkable apparition of the Blessed Virgin appeared to Bill at her home, according to Riche, as 'a woman sitting in an armchair. She was dressed in a variety of shades of blue, full flowing draperies and she wore a tiara-shaped crown with projecting rays that appeared to be jewelled with dull opaque stones like pearls and opals. She had dark hair and she began to speak. She spoke in Russian 'You have been a good cab horse to bring others to me. Now I want a ride myself...I want to come back to Liskeard.'

Being rather sceptical Bill replied; 'If you are who you seem to be, I need some sort of proof... I ask you to stay there long enough for me to make a sketch of you. Then tomorrow, I'll start painting a picture based on that sketch. I'll submit it to the Paris Salon, and if it is hung, which is most unlikely, I will accept that you are genuine and try to do something about your request'.'

Bill did a quick sketch on an envelope and the woman disappeared. From the sketch she produced the watercolour painting *La Vierge à la Porcelaine* and was entered for the exhibition in the Paris Salon where it was accepted and hung for two years.

When Bill started to research Liskeard's history she discovered that a shrine in honour of the Blessed Virgin had existed on a site in Liskeard called 'Ladye Park'. The records from the thirteenth and fifteenth centuries stated that the pilgrimage spot was situated in a clearing between two woods: 'one with deer and the other without'.

Bill discovered the true site and the restoration of the shrine became her mission. Today an annual pilgrimage to Ladye Park is organized by the Cornish branch of the Ecumenical Society of the Blessed Virgin Mary. The work on the shrine brought her in close contact with Claire Riche, the Cornish author who catalogued the story in *The Lost Shrine of Liskeard: An Grerva Gellys a Lyskerrys* in 2002.

Even in her last years Bill remained a key part of the Cornish community, making friends regardless of age, race or background. One such friendship, formed in the 1970s, was with Michael Maine and in true style commandeered the young orphan as the last official member of Ferguson's Gang. In later years Maine was bestowed with the mantle of continuing the good work of the Gang. Upon her death Bill arranged for a letter to be sent to The Times by Maine (a copy is held within the National Trust archives) which included her final request:

'By tradition bandits make a final request before they go to their just reward and Bill Stickers lives and dies true to form.

'Having depleted all worldly goods in pursuit of Ferguson Gang activities, and others, he dies with one mission outstanding and therefore his final request is that the gang be opened to all National Trust members so that they may acquire Ladye Park in Liskeard Cornwall and preserve it for posterity. To this end he has appointed the first new member of the Gang who goes by the pseudonym Pegasus.'

Bill Stickers died on 13th November 1996 at Kenwyn Nursing Home, New Mills Lane, Truro. She left no earthly possessions yet her legacy of good works still continues to enrich us all today.

Sister Agatha

The Early Years

Brynhild Catherine Granger was born on 15th February 1908; part of a provincially important dynasty. Her father, Harold Granger, inherited the family business (and fortune) from his uncle at the turn of the twentieth century. The business was fruit farming, something the county of Sussex was famous for at this time. His business activities though were not confined solely to this; they also encompassed interests in the Southend-on-Sea property company.

The family were non-conformist free thinkers; Harold's aunt was Myra Sadd, the suffragette, who was sent to Holloway prison for two months after throwing a brick at the window of the War Office. She was force-fed and suffered a broken nose yet she was still determined to champion the women's cause. Her husband supported her fully, even writing to the Home Secretary to complain of the conditions at Holloway. This liberal approach to life gave Sister Agatha a far wider social vista than many of her peers enjoyed.

Her own mother, Isabella, worked for the charity Dr Barnardo's, where she was a House Mother for one of the local homes; through Isabella, Agatha was related to Charles Tattershall Dodd I and Charles Tattershall Dodd II, eminent artists of the time. Charles Tattershall Dodd I was her grandfather, an artist famous for Kent landscapes including 'St Helena Cottage, Tunbridge Wells'; 'Reynold's Farm'; 'Rocks with Cattle Grazing and Standings Mill, Broomhill'. One particular favourite painting of his was 'Isabella Rebecca Dodd feeding a ewe, ducks and chickens at Groombridge, Kent' currently displayed at Tunbridge Wells Museum and Art Gallery. This oil painting shows Agatha's mother as a young girl. Her grandfather and uncle had their studio at Grosvenor Lodge, Tunbridge Wells although both liked to paint outdoors whenever possible to capture their scenes in-situ.

Sister Agatha's father grew up in the family home of Hill House, Maldon where he and his mother lived with his elderly uncle Alfred and cousin Henrietta. When Alfred died Henrietta became the matriarch of the household and chose as her companion Miss Dodd. This connection between the Granger and Dodd families led to Harold and Isabella being introduced and eventually marrying at St John's Church, Tonbridge in 1904. The young family continued to live at Hill House where their two daughters were born; Isabelle in 1906 and Brynhild in 1908. The girls grew up amongst the bosom of the Granger family; they were a large extended sociable family who held prominence in the area. The family were photographed by Spalding in 1910 and her uncle painted a portrait of his sister with Henrietta.

Agatha attended the local grammar school before joining Isabelle at Saint Felix School, Lowestoft. It was here that her passion for music was carefully tutored and, while still at school, she was introduced to a friend of her parents, the famous composer Harold Jervis-Read. They began a correspondence which Jervis-Read fondly recalled in a later letter in 1929. 'It shall repose with one you sent me long ago from St Felix'. Jervis-Read was not the only male correspondent Agatha wrote to, she also liaised with Mr Wisbey from Leigh on Sea but he did not feature in her life after school.

It was at Saint Felix, in Bronte House, that Agatha formed two friendships, one with Red Biddy and the other was with her sister's friend Prascovia Shoubersky, who like Isabelle went on to study at Newnham with Bill Stickers.

The school fostered a sense of emancipation; as well as enjoying a later famous Head Mistress (Anne Mustoe cycled alone from England to India), other Saint Felix alumni include Baroness David, the Labour Peer who also attended the same Cambridge College as Bill Stickers; Lilias Margitson Rider Haggard, MBE, daughter of the British writer, Sir Henry Rider Haggard, of whom she wrote a biography; and the Eastenders' actress Hannah Waterman (daughter of Dennis Waterman).

Although the family were immensely wealthy (Henrietta left the modern day equivalent of two and half million pounds), both Agatha and Isabelle were expected to earn their living once they had completed their university education.

Miss Silcox, the Head Mistress at Saint Felix had suggested that Agatha did not follow Isabelle up to Newnham, instead Agatha's mother made enquiries to King's College about the possibility of Agatha attending there instead. Two days later her father wrote to the College saying that Agatha 'knows two of your present students' and made the case for her to attend.

Education

Records at King's College show there was a flurry of correspondence. As preparations were underway for Agatha to attend King's, her mother and Henrietta Sadd decided to visit the Principal and inspect the college after which her mother wrote again to ask whether there was a piano available for Agatha to use as they wanted her to keep up her piano practice. The secretary responded: 'There are two pianos in the hostel... There would be no objection however, to your daughter bringing one with her if you wish her to do so'.

In October 1926 Agatha went to study for her Household and Social Science degree, staying at the Queen Mary Hostel in room number 19; at the end of the summer term she wrote enquiring if she could change rooms to number 17 if Miss Rodcliffe went down. During this vacation Agatha worked for the Warden's sister.

The next academic year was unsuccessful for Agatha, although passing the special intermediate examination she failed Household Work and the second BSc examination in 1928. This threw the family into turmoil, Agatha was determined to continue studying but the restudying would have meant her staying at King's for five years to complete a three year course. Her mother wrote of Agatha's distress 'Please do not tell her I have written only that I mind because on Saturday she was so terribly distraught and she is not one of the strongest'.

During this time Agatha had been suffering with her teeth and her uncle, Fredrick Lawson Dodd a dental surgeon, also wrote to the College explaining that she had cause to attend him over thirty times in three months due to the serious condition she was suffering from.

Her father contacted John Sargent, the Education Officer at Southend-on-Sea who wrote to the College trying to establish what Agatha's options were; her sister Isabelle also begged an appointment with the Warden: 'If all the plans with regards to my sister's future are in the melting pot I wonder if I could come and see you regarding them some day next week?'.

Agatha took the time over the summer to consider what to do and decided to take up the offer of a two month trial with The Charity Organisation Society which, if she was a satisfactory candidate, would then sponsor her to take the shortened course for an Almoner's training. As a result of this Agatha still remained linked to King's but moved out of the hostel. 'I have taken a room in Airlie Gardens' she wrote, becoming a lodger at the same boarding house as Lord Beershop. At this time Agatha applied to The Institute of Hospital Almoners based on a two day try-out as an Almoner at St Thomas' Hospital that summer. Her placement with The Charity Organisation was satisfactory and in 1929 she attended the London School of Economics to study the theoretical part of the Almoner training.

Although Agatha did not complete her degree, the recommendation she received from King's College was still glowing. 'She is hardworking, public spirited and has the kind of presence required for interviewing'; her attitude was such that it would allow her to strike a happy balance between credulity and scepticism in relation to patients.

Joining the Work Force

The move from a totally academic degree to a more hands-on subject suited Agatha, although Jervis-Read was a little less convinced. He wrote 'Are you an ALMONER yet? Do you get a sort of holiday?' He was also solicitous of her, 'It seems dreadful you should be 'nearly a real almoner'. I think you'll always remain Brynnie in spite of almoning but you'll have to be very careful'. Her Almoner training began with The Royal Free Hospital, she then worked at The Elizabeth Garratt Anderson Hospital on Euston Road in 1929 for two years, before travelling the country finding placements, firstly at Norwich Provincial Hospital in 1930 and then at The General Infirmary, Leeds in 1931.

Her first permanent job was in 1932 back at The Royal Free Hospital where she had trained, joining the team as an

Assistant Almoner. In 1934 a new and exciting opportunity was offered to her, a year's appointment as an Assistant Almoner at The Melbourne Hospital, Melbourne, Australia. By this time her father, anxious about his daughter's complex attachment with Jervis-Read, encouraged her to go and she duly left England for a year, having enjoyed a brief holiday before she went with Bill on the Scilly Islands.

This period from 1928 to 1934 was a traumatic time for Agatha; not only was she dealing with her own complicated love-life but she was expected to act as mediator between her warring parents as well.

Lovers and family

Her correspondence with Jervis-Read, which started at school, had extended into a physical relationship. The main issue with this was Jervis-Read was 29 years her senior, married and had five children. The letters between them are fraught with passion; full of recriminations, declarations of love, ardour and demands for attention. Agatha took to addressing Jervis-Read by the pet name of Fitzroy, after his address, as a term of endearment; trying to carve out something special that she did not have to share with Marjory, his wife.

The letters show a curiously personal side of Jervis-Read that was kept hidden from so many others. The Royal Academy of Music magazine, In Memoriam, contains a description from one of his students: 'In the eyes of a 9 year old he was a superior being and that feeling has never faded. A certain aloofness of character has prevented most of those with whom he came in contact from knowing the real man, who was simple, widely cultured and most loveable.'

Yet this older, insecure, married man held a continued fascination for Agatha that refused to be doused, despite the fact she was not the first lover he had taken. 'I have had two 'serious' loves as you know.' He told Agatha but to paint him as a philanderer would be incorrect. The marriage to Marjory had been failing for some time; his wife was conducting her own affair with Dr Wells and in fact went on to have a child with her lover. Ironically, although Marjory was not faithful to Jervis-

Read, she wrote to Agatha advising the young lady to look elsewhere for a husband as Jervis-Read was neither available nor reliable.

Agatha took this advice to heart and broke the relationship off several times, but it was hopeless. Jervis-Read would implore her to change her mind and in the end she always did. His love for her never failed though, he even organised for Agatha to have a piano while living in London and gave her Miss Dougal's old one. When the opportunity in Australia arose he was distraught at the prospect of her going. 'You are willing... to give up the London you love, your friends, perhaps everything you love, for no reasons I can see except sheer self-strangulation'.

As her departure got nearer he declared that he would follow her there if necessary, 'You go to Australia. I shall come, I know, I shall somehow even it means giving up all that I have.'

Despite the emotional blackmail Agatha went to Australia, returning a year later, and things began to follow in the same pattern as before. The Granger and Jervis-Read families throughout this time were on calling terms; making it a strangely volatile situation. Isabelle, Agatha's sister, would be invited to afternoon tea with Marjory; Jervis-Read would stay at Hill House visiting Agatha's father. This claustrophobic relationship must have intensified Agatha's concerns about the viability of any long-term future with Jervis-Read, particularly when the situation with her parents was worsening.

The differences between her steady business-headed father and her artistic mother had grown to such disproportionate proportions that they were irreconcilable; they were living apart, Harold at Hill House and Isabella at Gordon Mansions, London. The situation was unbearable for both and the couple took the unusual step of becoming legally separated. In 1932 Harold Granger became separated from his wife; the terms of the separation saw them living apart as if she was unmarried; that neither annoyed, disturbed nor interfered with any members of the family; and that neither was required or compelled to cohabit with the other. In return Isabella received £29 3s 4d less tax a month for 1934, £31 5s less tax a month for 1935 and £33 6s 8d from then onwards. She would also have all her wearing apparel and personal ornaments. It was signed by Isabella and witnessed by her sister-in-law Edith Tattershall Dodd.

During this time both parents made demands upon their two daughters; Agatha wrote rather wryly to Jervis-Read that 'Mummy is staying here as she has left Hill House for good'. After the separation her father went on to form a relationship with Sylvia Fillmer, a young lady from Oakfield, Hurst Road, Hassocks. When Harold died on 6th February 1936 he bequeathed a small legacy to Miss Fillmer (in the shape of 200 shares in the Southend-on-Sea Estate company) to be overseen by Sister Agatha as trustee.

This emotional roller-coaster did not turn Agatha off the idea of marriage though; Jervis-Read finally succeeded in securing a divorce from Marjory allowing the two of them to get married at the Westminster Register Office on 5th May 1939. It was witnessed by Cherry Morris and Peter Latham; Harold was 60 years old and Brynhild was 31.

They honeymooned at Ye Olde Swan Hotel, Brightingsea, Essex, just down the coast from Hill House before moving into Jervis-Read's house on Perrins Walk where Agatha took some time off to enjoy married life. Although Agatha had no children she became a second matriarchal figure for Jervis-Read's family, indeed she took care to stay in touch with her step-grandchildren wherever they lived. One of these, Diana Jervis-Read, fondly recalls how Agatha would want to hear about her granddaughter's latest news rather than dwelling on herself. 'She was a wonderfully kind person who was always there for you'.

The advent of World War II saw Agatha, like the other Gang members, doing her bit working for the Red Cross. She joined the Emergency Help and After Care Department for Invalided Ex-Service Personnel in February 1944. By 1948 she had become a secretary becoming a Grade II Executive. During this time she revisited Australia, travelling on the Orion to Sydney and coming home via Colombo and Suez. Four years later she became a Serving Sister of the Order of St John finally becoming a Director in 1958, a post she held for over a decade.

In 1965 Sister Agatha's work was recognised when she was awarded an OBE in the New Year's Honours.

Music continued to play a major part of Agatha's life, particularly after her marriage. The young Geoffrey Parsons became her lodger when he arrived in England from Australia and together they held drawing room concerts and soirees for musicians of the day, with Agatha handing round dainty refreshments. Among those who attended was Dame Irene Ward (who also became her lodger in later years).

Ferguson's Gang was almost as great a part of Agatha's life as it was to Bill. She was an energetic organiser for the Gang's activities, liaising with the National Trust over various issues as well as keeping in touch with the individual Gang members socially. Red Biddy would often be invited over for dinner and Agatha also had Bill to stay when Uncle Gregory entertained a young German man in London for a week.

Agatha was quite frank about the Gang with her closest friends and family; her stories intrigued Jervis-Read and he demanded to know more about the fascinating Bill Stickers, although then exclaiming he found most of the Gang to be absolutely puzzling. When Agatha updated him on Lord Beershop's alternative religious studies he applauded her efforts: '[she] is clever. I studied Buddhism intently once but found it not satisfying'.

The Gang's headquarters obviously held strong memories for the two lovers; when the mill was first rescued by the Gang, Jervis-Read anxiously enquired: 'And is the 'appointed climax' reached?'. Then when he left Marjory, Agatha suggested he lived near Shalford and he diligently investigated moving out there. 'The mill is at Shalford, Surrey.' Agatha wrote. 'It's about a mile Cranleigh side of Guildford. Do go and see it one day. The architect living there is one John Macgregor, a most hospitable family. I'm sure they'd like you very much. I usually go down with the Gang, as they are already very generous to us. I slip in too when I go riding at Merrow.' However the distance from Shalford to his work at the Royal Academy of Music precluded such a move out to the country and he remained in London. Instead the pair used the mill for their romantic liaisons;

112

sending letters to set up the assignations: 'My sweetheart I wonder what you are doing today? Did you say you were going to the Mill tomorrow? Can't I too?' and the impulsive: '7.30 Mill – come, having tea... well you should catch a few fish today on the pond'.

Agatha, like Bill, continued to stay in touch with the National Trust. After her marriage she did enquire about the possibility of renting the mill to live at, however as the lease was still with the Artichoke's family, Agatha was never able to live there. Instead she began a correspondence with Matheson, the Trust's secretary over the possibility of buying another property, particularly when the Gang were unsuccessful in purchasing and saving The Old Pump House. Agatha was sent details of another house in Barkway but it was dismissed as too far away.

Agatha's marital home remained in London at Grosvenor Crescent Mews where in the early 1960s she rented out one of the rooms to friends including Fiona MacDermott and Dame Irene Ward, the Conservative MP for Tyneside. She and Harold did finally buy a weekend home, selecting a wonderful old thatched cottage at Aythorpe Roding, near to her childhood home. After Harold's death she could not bear to part with it, despite the impractical nature of the rambling property. Instead she converted the barn, allowing her to rent out the main house to friends. Here she regularly entertained with all her usual gusto and consideration, making her guests feel totally at home.

In 1989 she attended, without disguise, the celebrations at the Old Town Hall to commemorate the Gang's efforts. Agatha went along with her old friend Joyce Conwy-Evans, the famous designer, where they presented the National Trust with a collage designed and decorated by Conwy-Evans. During this visit Agatha exclaimed: 'It was always important to remain anonymous'.

After retiring Sister Agatha moved out of her flat; living with Gladys, her long-term secretary. She eventually moved out of London to Danbury, Essex where she died in 2004.

113

Red Biddy

The Early Years

Rachel Pinney was born on 11th July 1909 at Cheltenham Terrace, Chelsea, part of the Dorset-based Pinney family; owners of estates at Broadwindsor and Pilsdon and whose historic business ventures included, like Bill's family, extensive plantations in the West Indies, particularly on the island of Nevis. These had been run personally by members of the family, although there were some instances of absentee governorship from Racedown and Bristol. The family's business had been headquartered in Bristol with substantial property interests in the city and surrounding Somerset. However by the time of Biddy's birth her father owned an estate at Racedown, serving in His Majesty's Army.

Red Biddy's father was Major-General Sir Reginald John Pinney KCB. He served as a British Army officer who was immortalised as 'the cheery old card' in Siegfried Sassoon's poem 'The General'. While most of his officers in 1916 felt him to be 'pleasant and human' some of his methods caused unpopularity in certain quarters. By stopping the regular issue of rum and replacing it with tea, one NCO rather cruelly described him as a 'bum-pinching crank, more suited to command of a church mission hut than troops'. He was a highly disciplined individual, a tee-totaller who did not smoke and was devoutly religious. It is no wonder that the headstrong Red Biddy rebelled against such a character.

After the Great War he retired to Broadwindsor where he was a Justice of the Peace, a High Sheriff for the county and a Deputy Lieutenant (supporting the Lord Lieutenant of Dorset – Anthony Ashley-Cooper, 9th Earl of Shaftesbury). He also retained links with the regular Army, serving as Ceremonial Colonel for the Royal Fusiliers, his old regiment, from 1924 to 1933. In addition he held an honorary Colonelcy of the Dorset Coastal Brigade, Royal Artillery and 4th (Territorial) Battalion of the Dorset Regiment.

Red Biddy's mother, Hester, was from a similar wealthy family living in Middlesex. Hester's father was a Lloyds underwriter who had five children, four sons and a daughter, all of whom were successful in their own right.

The family were Quaker and no doubt this shared religious dogma was one of the attractions which Reginald found in Hester. Her family home was Great Buckingham House, Stamford Hill; the interiors of which were personally designed by William Morris. Growing up exposed to the simplistic charm of the Gothic designs no doubt influenced Hester's appreciation of the Arts and Crafts ethos and something which her daughter went on to inherit.

Hester and Reginald were married in 1900 at Old Shoreham, Sussex. They had three daughters and three sons, Hester, Bernard, Mary, Robert, Rachel and John; Red Biddy was their fifth child. Although her parents appear not to have been strict disciplinarians with their children, their religious approach, her father's views on abstinence and their politically conservative nature were at total odds with Biddy's own nature. She did, however, flourish from the almost daily contact the family had with the literary world at the family home at Racedown. In fact the house had been rented for a short time to the poet William Wordsworth and his wife.

The family were related to EV Lucas, the biographer of Charles Lamb and good friend of Edwin Lutyens (bringing Biddy into contact with the famous early 20th century designer). Lucas was responsible for teaming AA Milne up with EH Shepherd for the Winnie-the-Pooh books. Indeed if he hadn't then the Gang's headquarters may never have been immortalised in the Pooh-Sticks illustration.

The Pinneys were also in close communication with Thomas Hardy whose house, Maws Hill, was neighbouring onto the Racedown estate. There was an additional literary link through Hester's brother, Biddy's uncle Henry and aunt Ruth.

Henry was an eminent physician with a deeply romantic appreciation. In later life he was a poet, becoming firm friends with Thomas Hardy and a mentor to Siegfried Sassoon; perhaps the fondness for his mentor encouraged Sassoon's poem 'The General' to be so favourable towards Biddy's father.

Henry married Mary Ruth Mayhew in 1904; she was a published author in her own right with two novels, *Compensation* and *A History of Departed Timings*, a collection of Thomas Hardy's works and a translation of *Der Kleine Tod* or 'The Little Death' by Irene Forbes-Mosse.

The close relationship between the Hardys, Heads and Pinneys and their conversations around current affairs meant Biddy would often hear Hardy expostulating about the value of the Society for Protection of Ancient Buildings. He was a committed SPAB caseworker, working particularly hard to protect churches in the West Country. Hearing this orator passionately championing the case for preserving England's historic buildings laid firm foundations for the future Ferguson's Gang. When Bill Stickers suggested the formation of a band of friends to support the National Trust, Biddy was only too ready to join the call to arms.

Hester's family had a strong influence (both positive and negative) on Biddy; her uncle Christopher joined his father as an underwriter at Lloyds before becoming a Conservative party Councillor and Mayor of Chelsea from 1909 until his death aboard RMS Titanic in 1912. Biddy rebelled against this conformity to a middle-class ethos and joined the British Communist Party, swelling the ranks of titled and wealthy young women supporting the cause which included The Hon Jessica Mitford and Silvia Pankhurst.

A more benign and long-lasting influence was her uncle Henry, who discovered Head-Holmes Syndrome and Head-Riddoch Syndrome. Red Biddy was fascinated by his pioneering work into the somatosensory system (i.e. the receptors and processing centres required for touch, temperature and pain) and the sensory nerves.

Henry's work provided the catalyst for Biddy's future career. Her prep school education was at a private school in Swanage before being sent to Saint Felix School where she met Sister Agatha. From here she naturally went to Bristol, the university nearest her family home, to study medicine. She appeared on the university calendar between 1928 and 1930 as an

116

undergraduate in residence. Although she passed her immediate exam for the BSc in June 1929 she did not finish her degree.

Determined to pursue her dream of a career in medicine she then followed in Sister Agatha's footsteps and went to King's College in 1931, having passed the matriculation earlier that year to gain entry. She lodged at Lansdowne Crescent while studying for a medical degree and for the first half of the course she passed her exams including physical chemistry, special physics and pure maths. However during the summer of 1934 she was absent for most of the term and the following year she failed her physics exam. Her tutor recommended that Biddy contacted the Dean (Professor Griffiths) for a letter of exemption on medical grounds which she would support; however in the August her studies at King's were cancelled and Biddy once again left university without a degree.

Biddy's stature was short and squat; throughout her life she had suffered from erratic illnesses. In her correspondence from school to her father she wrote about it being unfair on having to miss out on games because of Matron's worries about her health. The condition was never clearly diagnosed but continued to trouble her.

Marriage

Of course it was not necessarily just the old problem with her legs that caused this interruption of her studies. During 1934 Biddy, rather daringly, left Lansdowne Crescent and moved in with her lover Luigi Cocuzzi. They lived together before getting married in November of that year, setting up home in Danvers Street, Chelsea only a couple of roads away from the Pinney's London residence.

Luigi was a master cabinet-maker of Italian descent, although he himself was a British citizen; Luigi's father was the musician, Michaelangelo Cocuzzi, who had previously been a master cabinet-maker. The family lived in the area of Mile End; the East End at this time was a popular spot for immigrants and refugees. Luigi had grown up with a bohemian lifestyle, something which was an antithesis to Biddy's family.

117

They set up a company together 'Cox and Pinney' designing and selling furniture. One of Biddy's male friends (and one who Luigi always considered to be a rival for her affections) rather waspishly wrote: '...and that the public buttocks are beginning to realise their need of that comfort which only Cox and Pinney can supply'.

They were married at Chelsea Registry Office on 10th November 1934 witnessed by two friends, Margaret Whytock Roberts and Margaret Cockerell, also from the East End. It appears no family were present from either side. Her marriage was yet another rebellious example; her siblings had found far more suitable partners, her elder sister Hester married Basil Marsden-Smedley and her brother Bernard married Rosemary Segrave.

The couple were beset by financial difficulties for most of their time together; in fact things became so bad that they were forced to take up Biddy's parents' offer of financial support to simply pay their bills.

Although the liaison might have been deemed 'undesirable' in the eyes of her parents, there can be no doubt of the sincerity of Luigi's love for Biddy in those early years. His letters expressed deep affection for her; missing her when they were apart and longing to meet up again. 'It was grand to hear your voice on the phone,' he told her; 'It will be nice to be together in each other's arms'. He tried to be supportive when she was forced to leave King's; 'I have reread [your letter] several times and it gives me a kick to read it. One of these days my love you will be famous I can feel it'.

When they were expecting their first daughter he was full of concern for her; 'I hope you are taking it easy my love because I want you to get strong and well so that our little Karin will be hale and hearty when she arrives'.

With Biddy's reoccurring illnesses, there was obvious concern for her health during this pregnancy; the pair moved into the Pinney's Chelsea house so that Biddy would have full time care and Karin was born on 23rd March 1936.

Then when Karin was a young baby and Luigi was staying away at the Central Hotel at Lyme Regis, he wrote to hear how Biddy and Karin were faring. 'I hope all goes well with Karin, the house and shop.' They were obviously concerned that Karin was not putting on weight as he counselled her to '...take her to the clinic. Maybe she wants something in addition to a whack on the breasts'. This was a reference to Biddy's preference for breast-feeding, something which shocked society in those days, particularly when she fed Karin out in public.

The next year Biddy moved into a farm labourer's cottage in Shalford with her baby, however choosing to live in a basic cottage with no servants, limited sanitation and no house-husbandry experience raised the concerns of her neighbours; especially as Karin continued to be underweight. There was also a suggestion that Karin was also suffering from rickets, possibly something inherited from Biddy, and she was adopted into the Pinney family to be brought up. Despite her removal from Biddy and Luigi, Karin retained her surname, eventually training as a Secretary and sailing out to the States in 1959 on the Ryndham where she eventually settled.

The relationship between Biddy and Luigi was never straight-forward; Biddy was looking for a career within medicine and Luigi was far more artistic. The break-down of their marriage was not helped by Biddy's infamous temper. When a later relationship failed Biddy showed tendencies of a 'woman scorned' scrawling pages of recriminations and accusations, the language passionate and bitter.

They had moved house constantly, something Biddy continued to do for the rest of her life, forever the nomadic rebel. They moved so often in the first years of marriage that Luigi was still listed at his father's house on the electoral register as a consistent address.

During the war Red Biddy stuck to her communist principles; the second Boo records her helping Jewish refugees who had fled Germany to become settled within London. Prior to war being declared one of Biddy's friends, Diana, had become concerned at the labour camps in Germany and had gone out to volunteer. Her regular correspondence with Biddy gave an insight into life in the camps which stirred Red Biddy into action to be involved with helping Jews against persecution by the Nazis.

As the war continued Luigi changed his name by deed poll from Cocuzzi to Cox, perhaps the Italian connection felt too uncomfortable being a British citizen with a foreign name. 1945 was a watershed year for the pair. As well as Luigi changing his name he also became the sole legal guardian for Peter who changed his name to Pinney-Cox. The same year Biddy, who had by this time finally graduated with her LRCP qualification from a West London University, reverted to using her maiden name and began to practice.

During this period they moved away from 93 Oakley Street, SW3 and onto the Fulham Road whilst also renting Beechlawn in Alton but it was a fractured time. In correspondence between them Luigi made reference to Peter and Karin along with another daughter 'Gina'; however no records show details about her birth. Like so much of Red Biddy's life, it looks like this was yet another unconventional situation. Even the birth of their final son, Christopher in 1948, was shrouded in confusion. Although Red Biddy and Luigi were divorced, Biddy went on to give birth to their son Christopher just days before Luigi remarried to Mary Waller; rather ironically at the same registry office where he had married Biddy.

Red Biddy's diaries show that she continued to stay in touch with Luigi after the divorce presumably so that she could organise for Peter to visit and stay with her. These visits were marked up carefully and he is mentioned in letters to friends. There is no mention of Christopher or Karin though; possibly she was estranged from them.

Politics and Medicine

After qualifying as a GP, Biddy turned all her energies into her career, bringing Luigi's earlier prophesy of being famous into a reality. Her social conscience meant that she was often looking to help David against Goliath and continuing to hit out at the establishment, just as she had done with Ferguson's Gang almost two decades before. Her political view tempered slightly after a visit to the USSR but she remained politically active, becoming a member of CND as the movement swelled in 1961.

Pat Arrowsmith recalled how during this time Biddy was one of the Direct Action Committee's band of tax refusers, campaigning against the Polaris nuclear submarines. She also participated in the demonstration walking from London to Holy Loch, the base for the submarines. When the demonstration ended with a seaborne attempt to board the supply vessel of the submarine the police, however, were already prepared. While the demonstrators were being hosed and arrested, Red Biddy manfully appeared on the scene, using her car which transformed into a boat to sail out and rescue her co-consipirators. Having painted the international Red Cross sign prominently on the vehicle she was able to act as rescuer unmolested by the authorities.

After this demonstration Biddy took to keeping silent on a Wednesday at a protest against nuclear weapons, communicating only by written notes. This caused huge complications, particularly when she appeared in court on the kidnapping charge. At the end of the 1960s she opened a peace café in Fulham and continued to be an active campaigner, attending Greenham in the 1980s.

Biddy continued her allegiance to the Communist Party throughout her life; she wrote in the Party's internal magazine, Focus, about a book she and her partner, Sarah Hopkins – the co-editor of *Greenham Common: Women of the Wire*, were writing with the working title *Obedience is a Sin*. At the time the pair were living between Ashburton, Devon and London.

While politics was the bedrock of her belief, becoming a GP was a major achievement for her and she practiced until 1961, the same year as she embraced the CND movement. For her though there was a void in the practical way she could really help individuals. Drawing on her childhood fascination of the sensory work of her uncle, Sir Henry Head, and perhaps trying subconsciously to rectify some of the mistakes made with her own children, Biddy set out to study child psychology under Dr Margaret Lowenfeld, the British-born pioneer of child psychology and psychotherapy. By the time Biddy joined the team at the

121

Institute of Child Psychology, Lowenfeld was already established as a world-authority on child psychology. Her research was taken up by doctors, therapists and social workers who used her techniques of Lowenfeld Mosaics, Lowenfeld Poleidoblocs and Lowenfeld Kaleidoblocs.

It was as a result of this encounter that Biddy developed a new approach to children's behaviour. She pioneered methods for conflict understanding which were called 'Creative Listening' and 'Children's Hours'. Ever astute, she saw the success Lowenfeld had enjoyed and created a limited company in 1967 to register her techniques which were subsequently taken up across the globe. One famous patient case from 1977 was a four year old boy suffering from autism in New York. This case formed the basis for Biddy's paper *Bobby – Breakthrough of an Autistic child* published in 1983. It is an interesting aside that her website still has a quote using the ancient Sanskrit word Lila (to play) to sum up her ethos, possibly a throw-back to the days of Ferguson's Gang and Bill Stickers, the Sanskrit scholar.

Her work was not without critics though and her professional reputation was questioned during the 1970s when she allowed her impulsiveness to take control and she was charged with kidnapping a fourteen year old boy, Matthew Collings. At the time Biddy was living between the UK and Ontario, Canada where she was a member of the Toronto Association of Individual Psychology and founder of the Children's Hours Centre at Toronto.

Reports of the kidnapping vary but Biddy strongly believed the youngster was crying out for help. Biddy had known Matthew for most of his life; being friends with his mother she had seen the boy spend seven years in council care during which time Mrs Collings had briefly lived in Biddy's London house. Matthew joined them at Biddy's house but when his mother was hospitalised he was sent to friends; he refused to stay, returning back to Biddy. Upon his mother's release he lived with her for three months before returning to Biddy once again.

Concerned for her young charge Biddy organised Alan Florence, a friend, to take Matthew to Canada and the two of them lived in a series of boarding houses for a month before being discovered by the Canadian police.

Biddy was unperturbed by events, despite the mother being frantic, and kept assuring Mrs Collings that Matthew was happy and could be produced within a few hours. The case was deemed serious enough for it to go to trial at the Old Bailey and Biddy was sentenced to nine months' imprisonment. In true Gang style, when the police arrested her for kidnapping she merely replied 'What fun'.

She continued to shock her family until the end, never conforming to their expectations; in 1989 she declared herself openly as a lesbian, although it was apparent from her correspondence that her affairs with women had begun decades before. She lived with her long-term partner Sarah Hopkins, flitting between their homes in Devon and London.

The daughter of Nancy Rose, an old Saint Felician school friend, remembered meeting both Red Biddy and Sister Agatha, recalling them as rather wonderfully eccentric characters.

Although her attitude and outlook differed to her siblings, Biddy remained in close contact with her family. Although her older brother, Robert, was by this time living out in New Zealand, she was a regular visitor to the others, calling in often several times a month.

Red Biddy died on 19th October 1995. She had lived her life according to her own moral code 'to find something only I can do and do it somewhat'.

The Bludy Lord Beershop of Gladstone Islands and Mercators Projection

Early Years

Ruth Christine Sherwood was born on 18th August 1907 to Wilfred and Bertha Sherwood. Like all the other Gang members her family were wealthy although they would have been classed as 'nouveau riche' compared to some of the others.

Wilfred's family originated from Penkridge, Staffordshire where they were yeoman farmers until 1805 when Wilfred's grandfather moved to Birmingham and established himself as a silversmith; this business flourished and the family moved to King's Norton. When Wilfred's father took over the business he moved out to Sutton Coldfield in 1870 where the family lived for the next century. Beershop's father trained within the family trade and he inherited the business, John Sherwood, on his father's death. The business was based at Regent Street, Birmingham and Ely Place, Holborn as well as having agents Hall & Russell on Upper Thames Street and Queenhite, London. Wilfred continued to run the business until the First World War when he sold it as a going concern.

On Beershop's mother's side, the Parkes had been manufacturers for over three hundred years, beginning with agricultural implements in the early 1600s. This was working in conjunction with a family relative, Dudd Dudley, the illegitimate son of Edward Sutton, 5th Baron Dudley of Dudley Castle, who was one of the first Englishmen to identify how to smelt iron ore with coke.

The business continued and in the next century saw it expanding to include a water-mill which was used in the production of spades at Sutton Park, an area which became known as Parke's Pool or Spade-Mill Pool.

After a while this venture faltered but fifty years later Francis Parkes re-established the manufacturing business in Birmingham where he worked with his friend, Sir Henry Bessemer, the engineer who developed the Bessemer process for the manufacture of steel. This process was used in the production

124

of steel digging forks, including heavy clay forks and D handled turnip forks, which slightly revived the family fortunes.

Francis' son Richard was Lord Beershop's grandfather; he married Ada Jane Fawcett (an Anglo-Irish lady) at the Wesleyan Chapel, Parsontown and in the 1880s they built Rathmore at Sutton Coldfield. The house was a large country home located between Rectory Road and Hollyfield Road with views over the wonderful rolling countryside. Richard collaborated with Joseph Chamberlain MP to found the Workmen's Compensation, after Chamberlain had successfully championed the Workmen's Compensation Acts of 1897 and 1899, setting it up as a not-for-profit insurance company. Richard was actively involved with politics and politicians until he felt forced to resign as a Sutton Coldfield Councillor when a case of municipal corruption was linked to the acquisition of the Riland Road gasworks.

Wilfred and Bertha (or Biddy as her family called her) were married in 1903. They lived at Woodlands, Whitehouse Common where Beershop, her two brothers and sister were born. The family lived here until Wilfred sold the silversmith business; then in 1926, when Richard moved out of Rathmore into a smaller house he had built in the gardens between the main house and the Boot Inn, the family moved into Rathmore and renamed it Derrymore.

The young Beershop attended the Edgbaston Church of England School for Girls with little academic enthusiasm; her reports from school show she was fairly idle although this was later put down to undiagnosed dyslexia. Her correspondence and notes characteristically show constant mis-spellings, supporting this late diagnosis. School was seen as a chore, particularly when she was labelled as slow and stupid; this may have been one of the reasons that art came to play such a large part of her life.

In the memoirs of Mary Bower she recalls how Lord Beershop would have been one of the last girls to wear the uniform of velvet-topped navy blue tunics worn well below the knee in winter; in summer the tunics were navy blue alpaca or linen with a thinner blouse. The regulation school hats were Panama hats with hat bands (red, green and pink stripes on a navy background). No jewellery was permitted to be worn and long hair was required to be tied back. Just before Lord Beershop left the fashion for short hair came in and the 1925 edition of the school's magazine had the poem 'Snip, snip, snip' dedicated to the new rage.

The school had 250 pupils with over 100 belonging to the netball club. As well as sports the theatre also featured heavily for the girls with the start of the Shakespeare Club; members were selected from the VI form and the best readers in the Upper School. They would meet once a week in the evenings to read Shakespeare's plays and was in addition to the traditional end of term entertainment. Knowing Lord Beershop's penchant for dramatics it would be no surprise if she had been an active member in both of these.

Of most interest to Lord Beershop though were the outings with Miss Blenkinsop, the art teacher; she organised sketching expeditions in the Cotswolds for the girls during the summer, using the wonders of the natural landscape for inspiration. For Beershop this was a relief from the drudgery of lessons.

The Edgbaston Church of England School for Girls firmly believed in the girls being involved in charitable works, something which made an impression on Beershop. As well as sponsoring a cot at Great Ormond Street Hospital, the same as Eversley School, they also took a more practical hands-on approach. The school adopted a deprived school from the Black Country, providing support and gifts to the disadvantaged pupils. The Head Mistress of this school enthusiastically praised the girls' efforts, extolling the benefits which her pupils received through this generosity.

Living for Art

It is unsurprising that Beershop and Bill Stickers became such intimate friends; both were highly artistic bohemians who had little regard for society. They were also part of some of the most illustrious political dynasties of the age. Bill Stickers within the Gladstone lineage and Beershop as a kin of Baldwin. Through her grandfather's political connections, Beershop was

126

acutely aware how Baldwin was persuaded to become involved in the National Trust through his friendship with Professor Trevelyan. In 1925, the family were only too responsive when Baldwin, along with Asquith and MacDonald signed a letter in The Times pledging support for the National Trust saving Ashridge Estate, Berkhamsted. This shared family conviction in the need to preserve England's heritage meant it was no surprise Beershop joined Ferguson's Gang so readily.

Beershop's artistic talents, along with her strong literary appreciation, were inherited through her father's side. Wilfred himself was a talented amateur artist and his mother was related to several famous authors. The family frequently conversed with their literary cousins including Rudyard Kipling, who bequeathed his home 'Bateman's' in Burwash, East Sussex on his death in 1936 to the National Trust. Elsie, his daughter and a contemporary of Beershop's, followed suit and bequeathed the copyright to Kipling's works.

The other literary connections of Beershop were the novelists Angela Thirkwell, her brother Denis Mackail and her son Colin MacInnes. Angela's godfather was JM Barrie, a friend of John Ferguson, who helped Angela to flee back to London after a disastrous marriage in Australia. Her return coincided with the formation of Ferguson's Gang and it is probable that not only was she aware of Beershop's involvement but her lively attitude would have whole-heartedly approved.

Just as Red Biddy grew up in a circle which included the design-greats of the time of William Morris and Edwin Lutyens, Beershop was directly related to the Victorian designer Sir Edward Coley Burne-Jones, 1st Baronet. Although he died a few years before Beershop was born his legacy as a British artist and designer inspired the young Beershop particularly with the local romantic associations conjured up of Burne-Jones and Morris bringing the Birmingham Set together to form The Brotherhood Society.

Like Burne-Jones Beershop studied art, however rather than attend the Birmingham School of Art as Burne-Jones had done, Beershop elected to enrol at the Slade School of Art. Her decision to opt for the Slade was probably influenced by her near

127

neighbours, the Tonks. Professor Tonks, at this time, was the fine art teacher at the Slade and lived in a large rambling Georgian house on the corner of Lichfield Road.

Henry Tonks first studied at Brighton and London Hospital before going to the Westminster School of Art under Frederick Brown. Tonks' pupils at the Slade included Stanley Spencer, Augustus John and Rex Whistler, putting Beershop in good company. Tonks' insistence on the visual truth of the observed world through the painted medium was a formative influence on Beershop's style.

Beershop enrolled at the University of London, University College's Faculty of the Arts on 4th October 1928; for two years she studied six days a week and paid £31 1s each year for fees. In the 1929 academic year Beershop was awarded the 2nd prize and received £2 for painting from a cast in the drawing certificate category. During this time Beershop's peers included Helen Lessore, who went on to run the Beaux Arts Gallery and whose style was very similar to Beershop's own, particularly when you look at the composition *Symposium*.

Beershop cut quite a figure at the Slade, with her Bohemian appearance of long skirts and her eccentric habit of smoking a pipe. However the latter was less of an affectation and more a practical consideration; rather than the bother of smoking a cigarette, which was fashionable at the time, the pipe allowed Beershop to have both hands free at all times for painting.

Beershop's family would often travel abroad at a time when this was still the privilege of the elite. In 1929 Beershop, together with her parents and sister sailed to Marseilles aboard the Rawalpindi, a liner finally destined for Bombay.

When she left the Slade, Beershop went on an extended holiday to Santa Maria, the capital city of Colombia. It gave her the ideal opportunity to soak up the colonial and republican architecture against the vividly colourful South American backdrop.

Soon after the South American adventure she went on a Caribbean cruise; sailing out to Bridgetown, Barbados on the Cavina, staying away for Christmas. On the way home she visited Kingston, Jamaica before finally returning home in March

1931 on the Camito, a passenger-carrying banana boat owned by Elders & Fyffes.

Returning to the UK Beershop found the country in the midst of the Great Depression, where unemployment was rising to three-and-half million and Britain's trade had fallen by half. She lived back in London at Cranley Gardens, working as a freelance commercial artist and for a while she successfully sold her work. As she continued to live and work amongst the artistic community though, Beershop began to feel uncomfortable at her cossetted lifestyle and her social conscience railed at competing against her fellow struggling artists for paid commissions. When an acquaintance was driven to putting her head in the oven through the despair of no work, owed rent and the struggle to find money even for food, Beershop took the decision to quit London, returning to Derrymore. Here she only ever painted for pleasure and never sought to pursue an artistic career again. It was during this period that she painted her only surviving self-portrait.

The War Years

As war broke out Beershop began working for a local family, the Owens of New Hall Manor, whose mediaeval moated house was built by the Earl of Warwick. She joined the Owens working at their factory, Brooke Tool Manufacturing, on the Warwick Road, Greet as her contribution to the war effort.

To make travelling to work easier, Beershop went to live with friends in Sparkhill; soon after though the German bombing raids began. The house she was staying in was bombed during the raids of October and November 1940; as well as this frightening experience Beershop also witnessed first-hand the true brutality of the blitz.

During the hot summer of the next year she recalled walking home from work and talking to one of the local rescue workers who rather ghoulishly told her 'We can't keep the bodies in this weather. Yesterday we buried one with two left legs'.

This had a profound effect on Beershop; she left the tool company and returned home to enlist as a driver for the Sutton Coldfield Ambulance Service. During the bombing raids the work was fraught and anxious, often working late into the night.

The women who made up the drivers and nurses at Hill Village and Boldmere formed a close knit group, hardly surprising when they witnessed so much pain and suffering.

Moral was kept high through the group's support; Beershop would sketch the teams and take photographs and, like Bill, recalled the cheering effect of poetry. She penned a few ditties including one which began:

'Sing a song of the Ladies at Hill –
Unless I'm mistaken they are sitting there still.'

It was written on a postcard which Margaret Wylie, Beershop's dear friend, cherished. Wylie was a nursing auxiliary at Hill and lived just down the road from the Sherwood's home. The family were also extremely wealthy and she was involved with charities and good works after she left school.

Other women of the Ambulance Service included Rosalind Strover who was married to Sutton Coldfield's curate. She stayed at the Sherwood's house on the worst night of the Birmingham blitz having gone to the Birmingham City Orchestra's recital as a deputy to the original viola player.

Fellow artist 'Leakie', Margaret Leake, was also a driver with Beershop. She lived in Tudor Hill and was as outlandish in her attitudes as Beershop. She had been adopted by Mr and Mrs Ansell in later life and upon Mrs Ansell's death went on to marry Mr Ansell with whom she adopted a young boy. By profession Leakie was a fashion artist, working freelance and her work was used in advertisements within the Birmingham newspapers including some for Grey's Stores on Bull Street.

Mary Perkins was another long-standing friend of Beershop; she lived in Lichfield Road near the Tonks' house with her widowed father. Her near neighbour was Mabel Lyde, who lived with her mother. She, Perkins and Wylie were the closest friends Beershop had outside of Ferguson's Gang and they all joined the ambulance service together; there can little doubt that Beershop conscripted these three as members into the Gang.

The staff at the Ambulance Service was made up of full-time and part-time women; the teams comprised of a driver and nurse. During the night call-outs, and if there was a stretcher case, they would be assigned a male colleague to accompany the team. As the war progressed the bombing raids across Birmingham and Coventry lessened, so the ambulance teams' work began to involve transporting the elderly and pregnant women to and from hospital. During idle moments they would relax with crosswords, arrange a set for bridge or make gloves for the men on mine-sweeping. They also formed an acting troupe calling themselves 'The Mere Players'. Their performances were held at Mere Green Hall in aid of the Red Cross, Prisoners of War and the Merchant Navy. When the group performed 'Victoria Regina' by Laurence Housman (a locally born playwright and pacifist) Wylie and Beershop took centre stage as Queen Victoria and Prince Albert.

As the war came to an end Beershop was still involved with the ambulance service, ferrying patients to the Warwickshire County Lunatic Asylum in Hatton; a classic Victorian establishment. It was during these drives that Beershop first began to notice an increased pain in her legs and periods of acute numbness. The doctors diagnosed it as a form of anaemia, a condition which had killed her two brothers earlier. Although it was previously believed to be incurable, at the time of Beershop's diagnosis there was a new, virtually untried, drug being made available. Beershop decided to risk it and fortunately it turned out to be the cure for her fatal disease.

After the war Beershop had a short stay in London, living with Norman and Susan Shine at Cheyneys Avenue before moving down to Devon to be closer to Bill; like Bill she became a tutor, taking a post teaching art at the Adult Education Centre in Dartington. Whilst teaching Beershop began to experiment with more tactile art forms and discovered a love for weaving. She became involved with Leonard and Dorothy Elmhirst and their recreation of a rural community at Dartington Hall, the mediaeval hall built by Richard II's half-brother. The Elmhirsts also established a progressive education school, where Williams-Ellis had sent his children and something which obviously appealed to Beershop's view on schooling. As a mark of her friendship with the Elmhirsts, Beershop wove the altar frontal for the Chapel

131

whose intricate design contained Richard II's badge of the White Hart as a central theme.

By the 1960s Beershop was once again living in London, this time on the London Road, Barking with Arthur and Ruth Worwood; before moving to Gloucestershire, first to a house in Amberley, to be near her widowed mother and subsequently to Minchampton, close to her sister. Twenty years later she suffered a stroke and went to spend her final time at Northfield House Residential Home in Stroud. The anaemia which had plagued her whole life was one of the contributing factors to her death; she died on 27th September 1990.

Kate O'Brien The Nark

Early Years

Mabel Joyce Maw was born on 10th October 1907 in Shrewsbury to Arthur John (known as John) and Agnes Maw; she had one brother, John. Kate was baptised at St Chad's Church on 4th November 1907 by the Reverend Arkwright and her godparents included Mabel Bosville, an aunt living in Kensington.

The family lived at St John's Hill, Shrewsbury which her father leased from The Draper's Company; it was an old comfortable house, built in the early eighteenth century with pediment dormers in the roof, sash windows and a part-glazed panelled front door. The family lived here with their domestic servants until the mid-1920s when they moved to Moreton Coppice at Horsehay.

Kate O'Brien attended St Elphin's School, Derbyshire; the school was founded originally in Warrington in 1844 by the Hon. and Rev. Horace Powys before moving to Darley Dale in 1904. There is a suggestion in the school's magazine from 1925 (when Kate was there) that the Bishop had resided in the school at one point with girls still referring to a small, rather insignificant closet as 'The Bishop's Bathroom'. Whether true or not it would have appealed to Kate's sense of the romantic.

The school song would be heartily sung out at the end of each term by the girls:

'Gathered once more together
At the end of another term,
We'll set the echoes ringing,
With voices strong and firm,
We'll all sing together
In praise of those gone before,
And singing, remember with sorrow
The faces we'll see no more,'

It was a small select school, with just over a hundred girl boarders, active in sports and an outdoor life. Kate however did not embrace this physical side; she was never involved in the

133

lacrosse, netball or hockey teams. Instead she invariably retreated into a world of books and study, keen to be able to pursue a university career.

Her father was forward thinking in terms of girls' education. He was keen to see his daughter progress, perhaps because the family business was no longer the thriving establishment it had once been.

Kate, like Sister Agatha and Red Biddy, had suffered from various illnesses during her last year at St Elphin's and her father, in consultation with Miss Flood, the Head Mistress of St Elphin's, decided that Kate would benefit from an intensive one-on-one tutoring in preparation for her matriculation. During this time Maw contacted King's College, London to request their prospectus.

Escaping to University

The period around 1925 to 1926 was one of huge upheaval for Kate; as well as recuperating from her ailments, she was leaving St Elphin's to go and live with her aunt Bosville, in London. Here she commenced studies with Mr Marcy of Chancery Lane. At the same time it appeared that her parents were no longer able to continue living together in the same house. Her father took rooms at the nearby Park Hotel, Wellington where he resided for over a year. Kate may well have been slightly withdrawn during this time; acutely aware of her family's now precarious finances and missing the strong loving relationship of a mother. In fact Miss Flood, upon hearing Maw's decision to send his daughter to King's College, felt compelled to write to Miss Reynard, The Warden, giving a glowing character reference. 'She is enthusiastic and anxious to do well in Household and Social Sciences and she has every encouragement from her father'. There is a separate note which Miss Flood wrote recommending Kate as the most deserving student she had and whether Kate could be considered for a scholarship, perhaps thinking of Maw's financial situation. Unfortunately no scholarship was offered and instead Maw footed the bill of £60 per session for Kate's degree.

134

Records from the College show Miss Flood also requested delicately for Miss Reynard to keep a caring watchful eye on Kate during her first term, explaining: 'her mother had completely broken down and for years she [Kate] has practically no mother'. It is perhaps no wonder that the absentee mother caused Kate and her father to form such a close relationship.

Kate began her three year degree course in October 1926; there had been a concern raised by her father that Kate's matriculation results from the September examinations would not be available in time for the start of term. The Warden proposed that, should Kate fail, she merely retook the exams in January 1927, thus allowing her to start her studies immediately rather than delay for a year. This suggestion was speedily accepted by Maw.

In the first year of the degree Kate studied chemistry, physics, biology and economic history; in the second year she studied chemistry, economic biology, general biology, general economic, business affairs and book keeping, hygiene and household work. In her final year she studied applied chemistry, bacteriology, hygiene, physiology and household work.

During this time she lived in the student accommodation at the Queen Mary Hostel and would visit her aunt at Elm Park Gardens on her two weekends off a month as well as staying with her during vacations, not attempting to go home to her mother at Horsehay.

These weekends off were strictly kept; during February in her final year, her aunt wrote to the College Warden apologising for keeping her niece away from College for a few days, explaining that Kate had been suffering from a severe cold which her aunt felt would do better to stay in bed with. Mrs Bosville then requested an additional week-end pass for Kate so that her niece could stay and recuperate with her. The Warden's reply was firm and emphatic; no exception to the rule of only two weekend passes a month would be made, so Kate was forced to remain in College.

During her second summer vacation Kate made her first attempts at earning money, presumably to help alleviate the financial burden from her father. She signed up with an organisation 'Useful Women' based in Dover Street; this Organisation of Gentlewomen had been formed with the object of 'bringing into touch those who want certain kinds of work done with those who are ready and able to do it for others'. The type of work included cleaning, letter writing, household chores and sewing. As well as her household organisational skills, learnt through necessity by running the family home in the place of her semi-absentee mother, Kate's seamstress skills were first rate, often making outfits for friends.

Working for her living

Kate graduated with a BSc in the summer of 1929. Having enjoyed the final vacation she applied to various hotels for work as part of the housekeeping staff. In September she met with Francis Towle, the MD of Gordon Hotels, at the staff offices in Whitehall Place and records show she received a glowing reference from the King's College Warden: '...honest, sober, respectable, intelligent..'; after which she joined Gordon Hotels Ltd.

The first hotel she worked at was the Metropole Hotel on Northumberland Avenue, made famous by Bert Firman being the youngest band leader for the Midnight Follies Orchestra and it was here that he first met Edward VIII and they struck up a close friendship. The hotel was chosen by the English Rugby team in 1936 who, amazingly, beat the New Zealand All Blacks 13-0. Upon arrival, and in a mood to celebrate, they were somewhat perturbed to find the defeated New Zealand team were also there.

A number of private Gentlemen's Clubs including the Aero Club and Alpine Club used it as their base and King Edward VII, as Prince of Wales, also frequented the hotel, electing to reserve a Royal Suite on the first floor for private entertaining away from the Palace.

When the hotel opened it advertised: '...the hotel's location is particularly recommended to ladies and families visiting the West End during the Season; to travellers from Paris and the Continent, arriving from Dover and Folkestone at the Charing Cross Terminus; to Officers and others attending the levees at St James; to Ladies going to the Drawing Rooms, State

136

Balls, and Concerts at Buckingham Palace; and to colonial and American visitors unused to the great world of London.'

A few years later Kate moved to work for another Gordon Hotel, still in Northumberland Avenue, The Victoria. This was a promotion; The Victoria was a 500 bedroom hotel which was designed for American visitors; it was palatial and luxurious, giving visitors easy access to the City, the West End for shopping and to Parliament. It was ideal for those visiting dignitaries and business men who were travelling from the States with their wives. Little wonder the tips from her 'old gentlemen', which Kate was able to save to give to the Gang's cause, were so bountiful.

The advertisement for The Victoria proudly proclaimed: 'This magnificent Hotel is one of the Finest in the world; 500 Apartments, Public and Private Rooms and Baths, unsurpassed for comfort, convenience and elegance. Completely lit by Electricity. Passenger lifts to every floor.' The last two points are now common place but one hundred years ago they provided The Victoria with a real attraction for her discerning wealthy clientele.

Kate's next post was a move away from the hectic life of the busy hotel and to more sedate and refined surroundings; Isabelle, Sister Agatha's older sister, secured Kate a post at the school she was working at. Kate worked here for two years as a housekeeper, living in digs near to the school at Highgate Hill.

It is probably while she was living here that she met her future husband, Philip Gaze, but as no offer of marriage was immediately forthcoming Kate continued her career, writing to her former College and asking to be sent any vacancies which they may be aware of. She considered a role at Merchant Taylors School but dismissed it when she realised they were looking for someone with institutional experience in cooking cakes and sweets, something Kate had never done.

Her next application was to the Bergman Österberg Physical Training College in Kent; here she stayed for three years as housekeeper, during which time her beloved father died. Work at the College provided a solace though; it had originally been founded in Hampstead in 1885 and transferred to Dartford in

1895. Martina Bergman Österberg, a firm supporter of women's suffrage, set up the College to provide young ladies with 'female emancipation, social, economic and spiritual freedom for women', ideals which resonated with Kate as part of the Gang.

As the war broke out Kate became very aware of the danger; Dartford, with its armament factories, was a front line target for the bombing raids and a depositing area for planes not reaching central London. Kate was issued with one of the 27,000 regulation gas masks provided by the Government and attended the special lectures at the Market Street Clinic to learn about incendiary bombs and how to recognise different gas devices.

Despite the town being declared a 'vulnerable area', the College saw no falling off in student applications. They did take their own precautions though due to their locality near the Thames Estuary. The College built three large and palatial trenches running underneath their cricket pitch, although initially they had problems with the trenches flooding.

One of Kate's original responsibilities was organising the menus and doing the catering helped only by two kitchen maids, however when the kitchens were refurbished and the student numbers had risen to 170, the College agreed to Kate taking on a trained Head Cook and Cook's Assistant. Through a deep loyalty to her Mater Alumnus, Kate wrote to King's enquiring whether the College had any suitable candidates.

Throughout her life the contact with her old university and school was intermittent; although she attended the Commemoration Dinner with Sister Agatha in 1937 she applied for the tickets rather late, owing to only hearing about it after meeting up with Agatha. The Secretary rather wryly quizzed whether Kate had not yet joined the Association, as all dinner notices were sent to subscribers. Perhaps finances were too tight to stretch to the fee or she may simply never have got round to organising her subscription; it is unclear. However the same was true with her old school; it appears from St Elphin's Old Girls Newsletters that Kate never got round to joining that society either.

138

Weddings and children

Kate and Philip were married in the summer of 1940; perhaps Kate's proximity to the bombing raids prompted the proposal. In a break with tradition they were not married at the bride's local parish church due to the breakdown in the family relations, instead they were married at the Radlett Parish Church. This was the local church in the village where Philip's mother had owned a house and which upon her death was bequeathed to her husband. Harry let the newly married couple set up their marital home here while he continued to live at the family home in Camden, London.

Philip was an electrical engineer, similar to his father who was a chartered civil engineer, both professions which were in demand after the war as the country had to slowly rebuild homes, public buildings and infrastructure. Harry moved to Southern Rhodesia, now Zimbabwe, in his retirement years where he died at St Anne's Hospital. All his effects (valued at £60,000 in current values) went to his son Philip.

Having married slightly later in life than was usual at that time, Kate and Philip were considered 'older parents' when they began their family; Kate was 33 and Philip was 34. They had two sons, John and Henry, fondly named after their own fathers. Interestingly Kate chose to have both babies in London, despite the on-going war, rather than the safety of the Hertfordshire countryside.

In later life Kate continued to use the Gang's HQ for an occasional get-away, corresponding with the National Trust regarding the possibility of installing a lavatory; perhaps the Gang felt it was a little undignified for middle-age ladies to be without some kind of home comfort. Kate and Sister Agatha met up with the Trust's local representative to negotiate how the toilet could be fitted unobtrusively. Kate, concerned about the condition of the water wheel, also requested the Trust to look at replacing or repairing the broken fins.

She would often visit either for a solitary stay or to meet up with Sister Agatha and the pair would go riding round the Surrey countryside.

Kate remained estranged from her mother for her adult life; Agnes moved away to Stoke-on-Trent where she died at The City Hospital, Bucknell. Annie Bamford, a married woman friend, was left to administer the small amount of money left. No mention was made by Agnes of Kate or her brother John, even at the end.

The sorrow at never having a loving relationship with her mother continued to trouble her and this sorrow was increased when Kate's younger son, Henry, died aged only 37 while still living close to his childhood home at Cell Barnes Hospital. Kate died just two years later on 29th May 1983, still heartbroken at the loss of her child.

Chapter Ten: Conscripted Members

Looking beyond the inner circle, there were a number of 'conscripted subscribers' who not only helped the Gang to raise their levies but were also involved in the secret activities with the National Trust.

Erb the Smasher and Fred

One of the key supporters of the Gang was Bill Sticker's brother, Robert. Born four years after Bill he looked up to this fascinating, intelligent charismatic individual who was always willing to include her brother in her imaginary worlds.

Erb, like Bill, was born at the family's London home at Whitehall and was seven when his father purchased Nanhurst. He went to a small select boy's prep school which charged £150 per annum and catered for 60 students, before going to Eton College in 1920. The Head Master at this time was Cyril Argentine Alington who, like Bill's John Ferguson, was an ordained Anglican priest and a well-known author publishing over 50 books including a series of detective novels. Alington had attended Trinity College and this may well have influenced Erb's choice of university. Erb went up to Cambridge in 1925 where he was admitted as a pensioner at Trinity. He passed the qualifying exam in Mechanical Sciences in 1926 and the Mechanical Sciences Tripos (in the second class) in 1928, when he was awarded his BA.

It was during his school days that his father, John, died unexpectedly. His father's two brothers, Arthur and Ernest, were executors to the will, handling an estate which was worth almost five million pounds in today's money.

Erb continued to have a close relationship with the Gladstone family, after his father died his uncles sought to look after him and Bill and to help wherever possible. When Ernest died two years later Arthur and Erb were appointed as his trusted executors. Both Erb and Bill were very close to their cousin Hugh and his wife raised funds for the Gang's activities.

The death of John Gladstone meant Erb became the head of the household, responsible for the family's money and fortune;

141

it was he who provided the wedding dowry for Bill on her marriage to Uncle Gregory; his mother seemed to take no part in the finances except when she required large sums to support Bill's latest scheme.

Erb, like his cousin Wilfred, studied engineering at university and the pair shared a house in London with Black Maria's family. However Erb chose not to pursue engineering directly as a career, nor did he join the Gladstone family firm to become an East Indies merchant. Instead he chose to work in the paper industry, joining the firm Wiggins, Teape & Alex Pirie Limited where he worked on developing new paper machinery; this was at a time when the company was expanding into manufacturing coated papers, gummed papers for stamps, card material, abrasive bases for sandpaper and carton boards for food and milk containers. The company is referred to in the Boo, a scrawled handwritten note at the end of Erb's report on his drop of the booty apologies for it being written while at the paper factory.

Erb was based in the London offices, Aldgate, however he used the firm's Glasgow office as the 'post-box' for the correspondence with the BBC during the discussions about the broadcast appeal, ensuring nothing was immediately traceable back to the Gang. He even went so far as to travel up to Glasgow to make the appeal, of course heavily disguised.

It was perhaps inevitable that being so involved with the Gang it was here that he would find his future wife. He met and married Naomi Trentham, daughter of George Trentham, Public Works Contractor, whom Bill christened 'Fred'. They met through Lord Beershop and her Sutton Coldfield friends; Fred had grown up alongside Beershop, Perkins, Wylie and Lyde; she lived at Four Oaks close to her father's construction business at Wood Lane, until it moved to Rookery House in 1967.

Like most of Beershop's friends, the Trenthams were wealthy; upon George Trentham's death the family had a country home in Shropshire, a London residence on Portland Place and the estate was worth nine million pounds in current values.

Fred became one of the conscripted members of the Gang through her friends and her husband; she certainly knew about Erb's involvement.

The family were avid sports-people; Erb was a keen skier. He was part of the exclusive Downhill Only Club who met at the Regina Hotel, Wengen for the season and attended the annual dinner at the Savoy. Fred was a keen tennis player, playing at Wimbledon between the years 1927 and 1937, despite becoming a married woman and starting a family with Erb.

Erb and Fred had three daughters, Kitty, Jean and Anne. The family grew up in Surrey not far from Erb's childhood home at St George's Hill until Erb's death. He died in St Peter's Hospital, Chertsey after an operation on 22nd November 1981 aged 74.

Silent O'Moyle

One of the other key instigators of the Gang was Arthur John Maw, the deaf-dumb deliverer of the booty in 1934. Silent was the father of Kate O'Brien The Nark. Although he was christened Arthur John in 1867, he was always known as John to save any confusion with his father, Arthur. He was one of five children born to Arthur and Grace while they were living at Benthall.

Silent, in accordance with family tradition, was sent away to boarding school with his brother Henry; they attended 'The Cross' at Repton, Derbyshire, not far from where he sent Kate. The school was set up in 1559 on land formerly belonging to Repton Priory. Other famous alumni of The Cross include the children's author, Roald Dahl, and the television presenter, Jeremy Clarkson.

When Silent left school he joined the family firm Maw and Co, the business set up by his father and uncle, Arthur and George, in 1852. The venture had been financed by their father, John Hornby Maw, a surgical instrument maker who had made his fortune inventing a baby's glass feeding bottle.

During the late 1800s Maw and Co was one of the two most important tile manufacturers specialising in encaustic tile designs, not only within England but across the British Empire.

Their tiles were described as 'durable and beautiful production of medieval art, in every style, suitable for churches, entrances, halls, passages, conservatories'. It is no wonder when Silent and Kate were so immersed in the historical beauty of the Medieval Ages that they became so dedicated to the aims of Ferguson's Gang.

The Maws were considered to be good employers, like their larger local philanthropic neighbours, Bournville and Cadbury; taking on local people when the factory expanded including unmarried mothers and people from Beeches, the local workhouse. At Christmas time every member of staff received a turkey, goose, fowl or other seasonable gift from the Maw family.

When Silent married Agnes on 8th June 1899, he had recently been made a director of the company and the clerks, designers and foremen held a social evening to celebrate the marriage. The event was held at Severn House, Ironbridge, the home of Silent's parents; on the celebration day the factory was decorated with flags and they even fired cannons in honour of the married couple.

After the Great War the fashions and demands for the encaustic designs dramatically declined. The business for geometric and patterned tiles grew for bathrooms and hearths but not enough to keep the business going. Silent saw for himself the difficulties the business slowly began to suffer. At the same time his marriage to Agnes was beginning to fall apart. He was therefore determined to ensure his daughter achieved financial independence, without the need of a husband, which was why he pushed so hard for her to get into university.

His son John trained within the tile business, eventually becoming a potter. In 1922 he was presented with a gold medal by the County Borough of Stoke on Trent Education Committee having obtained the Pottery Honours Grade for 1921-1922. He was also awarded a first class honours. He remained the rest of his life in Shrewsbury, at the heart of the pottery making world.

Kate's involvement in the Gang led to Silent's introduction and initiation. He accompanied Kate to buy the masked disguises from Harrods, acted as a deliverer of the booty to the National Trust with the accompanying 'bottle of poison' and joined the Gang at The Dorchester for the dinner.

He remained in London after Kate had finished her studies, presumably to be near loved ones (Kate and his sister Rachel) after the irreconcilable breakdown of his marriage. Having given up the family home at Horsehay he never had his own permanent home again; he lived at the Cromwell Hotel in South Kensington for much of the time. His primary concern was always for Kate yet he never lived to see her married; he died on 6th June 1938 at the Mount Vernon Hospital, Middlesex. He was still suffering from financial difficulties, even though he left £200,000 (in today's money) in his will. Upon his death The Times published notice to all his creditors and other persons having claims on his estate to contact Silent's solicitors, RA Clarke & Son of Wellington Salop. Kate was left with only her memories of her loving father.

Black Maria

Margaret Ann Gladstone was born in Dublin to Gerald and Margaret Anne Fitzgibbon on 6th September 1871. The family lived at Merrion Square North and Black Maria was one of five children; they were all baptised at the parish church of St Peters, Clondalkin in Dublin.

Maria's father was a barrister who went on to become Lord Justice of Appeal in Ireland, making him the Rt Hon Lord Justice. Maria was introduced to John through her father's friend Edward Fairfield, who resided in London and was a near neighbour of John Gladstone's at Eaton Place. Fairfield worked as part of the Colonial Office in Ireland and Gerald would regularly visit; it was when the family accompanied him on such a trip that Maria was introduced to John Gladstone.

John and Black Maria were married in 1899 and they lived first at Whitehall Place, where their two children, Bill Stickers and Erb the Smasher, were born before moving to Cadogan Square in 1909.

This was the same year as Maria lost her father; the obituaries for Gerald show him to be highly intelligent and hard working. The Glasgow Herald called him 'a broad-minded councillor and an unselfish friend'. He remained active in the Church of Ireland, particularly in relation to St Peters where all his children had been baptised and the family regularly attended services. He was a distinguished member of the Masonic order and had become Chancellor of the United Dioceses of Dublin, Glendalough and Kildare.

Gerald provided a powerful role-model for Maria, she inherited his quick thinking and intelligence; unfortunately she was of a generation who was not encouraged to pursue an academic career and was something which she bitterly regretted. It was one of the reasons she was so keen for her daughter to have the chance of an education and Maria remained a driving force behind Bill's application to Cambridge and subsequent studies.

After John died in 1922 Maria sold the family house in Surrey and moved to The Briary, Freshwater on the Isle of Wight. The house was steeped in history, something which appealed to the romantic sensitivities of Bill and Maria. The Briary was the birthplace of Lord Tennyson's godson, Lord Somers and he would often visit the family there. It was also owned by the artist GF Watts who, commissioned by Dean Liddell of Christchurch, painted Prime Minister Gladstone's portrait when he visited the house. Perhaps it was destiny that the house Gladstone visited would become the future home of his nephew's widow.

While living at The Briary one of Maria's close neighbours, the second Lord Tennyson, presented 155 acres of land to the National Trust in memory of his father, the Poet Laureate. This land was just a mile from her Freshwater home and must have shown both Maria and Bill how the English countryside could be preserved through the National Trust. It also inspired Maria to begin donating money to the National Trust directly, outside of the large levies Ferguson's Gang made on her purse.

Black Maria lived on the island but she retained the London house for much of the time, allowing her to visit the metropolis as she wanted and providing a base for Erb when he was working in town. The island though was her home and she had an intimate knowledge of the area, which was how Ferguson's Gang became aware of the Old Town Hall and why

146

she was so quick to ensure that any further guarantees of money for the refurbishment were forthcoming.

Maria loved living at The Briary; however tragedy struck in March 1934 when the house was gutted by fire. Maria was away at the time and so missed the harrowing experience of seeing her home burn down in front of her eyes. The source of the fire was never known but it was first discovered within the roof of the building. The fire service attended promptly but the lack of water pressure meant the fire spread out of control and within three hours most of The Briary was a-flame. Volunteers and members of the emergency services worked with the fire service to finally control it while the servants worked hard to salvage the valuable contents from the ground floor rooms as well as some of the paintings from the upper quarters. Soon after this harrowing experience she quit the island, selling the site of the ruined house.

As Maria grew older so her reclusive tendencies increased, she no longer wanted London life and finally moved to be near her daughter in the late 1950s, turning her back on the luxury and grand living she had always enjoyed. Instead she copied Bill and chose a small worker's homestead, Carrick Cottage, to live in, getting up early each morning to swim in the bracing cold sea.

Her granddaughters recalled her as a 'brilliant woman, utterly frustrated by not having an education'. Maria died at the Epiphany Convalescent Home, St Agnes on 25th January 1962. Bill Stickers and Erb were left her personal effects which amounted to £90,000 in today's value.

The Artichoke and Wife of the Artichoke

John Macgregor was born on 2nd October 1890 and baptised at St Barnabas, Kensington one month later. His father was Archie Macgregor, the pre-Raphaelite style painter and sculptor who was a close friend and near neighbour of Lucien Pissarro.

The family home was Ashchurch Grove, Starch Green, near Shepherd's Bush; so called because it had once housed a laundry. The family lived here until they moved to Stamford Brook House, Stamford Brook Avenue in 1901.

The Artichoke attended the Linton House prep school at Notting Hill Gate before joining his older brother, Alexander, in 1905 at the Royal College of St Peter in Westminster, better known as Westminster School. Amongst the alumni are seven Prime Ministers, another famous architect - Christopher Wren, and AA Milne.

When the First World War was declared, the Artichoke joined the 28th (County of London) Battalion of Artists' Rifles, a volunteer regiment of the British Army. This was a particularly popular unit for volunteers and recruitment became restricted to those recommended by an existing battalion member. Over 15,000 men passed through this battalion, mainly from public schools and universities, giving the Artichoke a valuable network within the upper-echelons of society including Vita Sackville-West and her husband, Harold Nicolson.

In 1916 he was promoted to 2nd Lieutenant with the 5th (Cinque Ports) Battalion, Royal Sussex Regiment before being attached to the 7th Battalion of King's Royal Rifle Corps in 1917. He was promoted to Lieutenant in 1918 and served twice out in France; 1914 to 1915 and 1916 to 1918.

In 1918 the Artichoke married Janet Connell Udale, who was the Wife of the Artichoke and although he had returned from France his marriage certificate shows him forming part of the British Expeditionary Force, so potentially in line to be posted back out to the front again. The Wife of the Artichoke had been born in Lincoln, where her father was a woollen merchant; the family then moved down to London, living first at The Avenue, Acton; then Birch Grove and finally Spring Cottage, Church Road, Hanwell. The pair were married at Hanwell parish church, on 28th March witnessed by Stanley Udale (her father) and Ellen Macgregor (his mother).

The Artichoke was influenced both by his father's artistic appreciation for the Gothic and medieval influences but also by his mother's pioneering social spirit. These two aspects combined in the Artichoke to form an architect with strong

148

traditional values that sought to bring social benefits to all those living in his built environment.

After the end of the First World War, the Artichoke graduated as an architect, becoming an associate member of the Royal Institute of British Architects in 1919. He went into practice with AR Powys, eventually forming Powys and Macgregor Architects. In 1920 he joined Powys on the technical panel of SPAB and in 1924 turned his hand to teaching, becoming an instructor in Architecture at Kensington Technical College. In 1937 he was awarded the distinction of being a Fellow of the Royal Institute of British Architects.

He went on to become a dedicated member for SPAB; it personified his Arts and Crafts ideals and in return he influenced the society directly and indirectly. Some of the more unusual contributions to the Society included its relocation to Great Ormond Street as well as introducing Monica Dance to the members. Dance worked for Powys and Macgregor in 1931 then, upon Powys' death in 1936, Dance took over some of the administration side of Powys' Secretary to the Society role, becoming Acting Secretary during World War II and finally Secretary in 1949.

The Artichoke was a socialist, wanting to bring a quality of life to everyone. In the flats he designed for Bethnal Green and East London Housing Association in 1936 he cleverly included a five storey ziggurat or 'A'-Frame section. This stepped sectioning enabled the flats to be like stacked bungalows, each one having a generous open balcony and natural light; an inspiration which came from Henri Sauvage's 1925 apartment block for working class tenants in the Rue des Amiraux.

As well as a love for traditional architecture, the Artichoke was fascinated by engineering, one of the reasons he got on well with Erb. He regularly combined traditional cladding with innovative concrete frame constructions. One such example was at Rivercourt where, under the direction of Hermes, he designed a squash court for Naomi Mitchinson, the social pioneer with communist leanings, which had a loggia with concrete pillars and plant boxes blocked with pattern.

149

Four years later the Mitchinsons commissioned the Artichoke to adapt an existing range of stone barns into a village hall for their Argyll estate at Carradale.

The Artichoke worked on other social schemes, such as Bethnal Green and Ongar, however his most successful building is thought to be Lennox House with its pyramid design, built in 1934.

True to his ideals though the Artichoke enjoyed restoring traditional buildings, the reason he was so speedily conscripted into Ferguson's Gang; his philosophy was totally attuned to the other members. As well as the extensive involvement with the National Trust at Shalford Mill and The Old Town Hall, he also worked on a number of restoration projects for the Church of England, repairing and restoring, amongst a host of others, St Mary the Virgin at Berkley, Somerset in 1948 and the old parish church of St George, Esher in 1964.

The Artichoke and Wife of the Artichoke had four daughters: Janella, Penelope, Joanna and Sally; they lived in London on the banks of the Thames at Chiswick Mall, renting Shalford Mill as a weekend cottage until the Second World War when the family moved out of the capital.

In 1980 the Artichoke was awarded the Order of the British Empire for his long standing services to the field of architecture and conservation. Both he and his wife died in 1984; The Times carried his obituary in the May of that year.

Granny the Throttler

Ellen Macgregor was mother to the Artichoke. She lived at Stamford Brook House until she died in 1951 aged 93. Together with her husband, Ellen was a pioneer in social work, founding the Hampshire House Trust and Club, Hammersmith for working men. The aim was to provide a social and educational environment with physical pursuit activities combined with more literary ideals.

During the Boer War Granny actively raised money in support of the Boer women and children, so concerned was she for their general welfare. She also became an active suffragette and passionately believed in supporting causes. When her husband died in 1909, Granny created one of London's first infant welfare centres, starting off in a room in Ravenscourt Park.

She maintained the friendship with the Pissarros after her husband's death, keeping up the tradition of staging plays in the studio and her love of theatrical dramatics endeared her to the Gang. Pissarro's daughter Orovida, starred in one of Granny's pantomime as a princess, causing her father to call out gleefully 'fairies! fairies!'.

In her later years Granny was still an imposing figure, holding tea parties for her friends in the garden; a neighbour fondly recalls how the elderly ladies clung to the fashion of dressing in Edwardian style costume with large brimmed hats accompanied by a parasol so that the party looked somewhat reminiscent of the days of Queen Alexandra.

Great Uncle Gregory
George Francis Pollard was born in the summer of 1906; the family lived at The Red House, Wymondham in Norfolk which was famous for the manufacture of bombazines for mourning clothes. Gregory had one older brother, John Amyas Pollard, who remained living in Norfolk until his death in 1978.

Gregory's father, John Empson Toplis Pollard, married Julia Mary and having qualified as a solicitor set up practice with his partner on the Prince of Wales Road, Norwich. The firm was a partnership between Richard Gourney Ferrier and John Pollard called Bignold and Pollard, however on 4th January 1936 Pollard took sole ownership of the business. Amongst his work was acting as liquidator for the Norwich Crape Company Ltd in 1924 and as executor for The Rev. Laurence Gifford Pollard, Uncle Gregory's uncle, of Brondesbury Park, Willsden in 1929.

During her early married years, Gregory's mother lived in Guildford Place, London as a boarder and was stated as living on her own means. There was no explanation why she was living away from her husband at this point or how she had money of her own.

The family moved to Norwich, living at Lansdowne House, the former Mayor's residence, an imposing 18th century house. Uncle Gregory attended Gresham school before going to Cambridge to study law where he met Bill Stickers.

He matriculated on 21st October 1924, having been admitted to Trinity Hall where he originally studied for the Law Tripos, presumably to follow in his father's footsteps. However, the law was not for him; he was only awarded a 3rd in the Tripos Qualifying examination in 1925. He turned to his favourite subject and switched to studying for a degree specialising in History and English.

He remained at Trinity where he studied with Arthur Elton, Bill's one-time fiancé. The two men shared an interest in literature and films, something which stayed with both of them for most of their lives. Gregory took the examinations for his 'Specials' in History in 1926 and English a year later; Gregory eventually graduated with his BA degree on 19th December 1927.

Gregory married Bill in 1928 and the pair lived in Dean's Yard. In 1930 they moved down to Cornwall and Gregory began writing a series of books which took inspiration from the Gladstone family's East India business. They were set in Georgian England and Colonial America; combining swash-buckling antics with a gritty reality. He was published in both the UK and America with publishers Grant Richards, Constable & Co and Little, Brown Company. His titles included Virtue Undone (or The Carefree Smuggler) in 1930, Slaves in 1931, East Indiaman in 1935 and Privateer in 1938.

In Virtue Undone he includes a touching inscription to Bill apologising for the story containing the racier aspects of the time; as always the question of sex raised a complex point for the couple.

Gregory designed the frontispiece linocut for Gamley Woolsey's books when she came to live in Welcombe, a skill he also used for the Gang to produce their Christmas card.

Like Bill he corresponded with major players in the literary world of the time; John Cowper-Powys, the novelist, was in contact with both Gregory and Gerald Brenan, Woolsey's husband; introduced through John's brother, the Artichoke's business partner AR Powys.

In 1935 Gregory plotted a journey aboard 'Seaplane', a Brixham built trawler which he had converted into a yacht, accompanied by Alan Gascoigne Sinclair and NR Cox. They departed from Falmouth and sailed over to Halifax, Nova Scotia. This trip was more successful than his earlier sailing trip to Norway when Bill accompanied him; on that occasion the boat sank. The only good thing that came out of the trip was Bill being able to buy her infamous wooden clogs.

At the start of the war Gregory presented a number of nautical paintings to the Falmouth Art Gallery on permanent loan. Two were by William Ayerst Ingram; 'Schooner on the high seas' and 'The home port – Falmouth'; the third was an engraving by Richard Wright 'The Fishery'.

When war was declared Bill threw herself into the Women's Land Army and her obsession with goats; Gregory, with his love of sailing, naturally enlisted into the Royal Navy as a volunteer reserve. He attended HMS King Alfred; not a ship but an RNVR officer training school at Hove, Brighton. At one point in the war German propaganda claimed to have sunk the land-locked HMS King Alfred – much to the amusement of the attending cadets. Here Gregory came to graduate as an officer where he would attend the mess on Thursday night for the formal dining-in evening which was accompanied by generous quantities of port.

While he was here Gregory was billeted into a former girls' boarding school, along with a Davis Cup player, a well-known yachtsman, Lord Selden and AB Horne, the producer for the Westminster Theatre, London. They slept in the dormitories with remnants of the girls' school around them, including a buzzer above each bed with a sign saying 'Ring for Mistress'; something which certainly generated a few raucous jokes between the men.

On becoming an officer he served aboard HMS Pearl, an anti-submarine trawler before joining the crew of HMS Globe II, a minesweeping whaler. From 1942 to 1943 he was aboard HMS Scalpay which acted as an escort and minesweeper trawler; he was based at HMS Boscawen, proving handy for Gregory to meet up with Bill when on leave. He was then assigned to HMS Sumar for the last two years of the war, a far more demanding role aboard the minesweeper trawler.

The war brought a number of discomforts, major and minor, for many; one of Gregory's was how to use the regulation gas mask. He had great difficulty in getting the rubber mask over his thick black beard which was over six inches long. The answer was ingenious. Bill and Gregory were interviewed, appearing in The Barrier Miner newspaper where Bill described their inventive solution.

'I parted my husband's beard and curled each section round a rubber hair-curler, so that it was fixed tightly under the chin. Then he put his face in the respirator, which fitted snugly round chin and curlers. When the curlers are taken out the beard is luxuriously waved. I think this is an added attraction.' There was a warning to any men who tried this; they needed to start curling the beard up as soon as the siren went as it took some minutes to pack it into the mask.

After the war Gregory became known locally at Cap'n Pollard, an image enhanced by his pirate-like beard and tall broad build. He became involved in politics briefly, becoming a Conservative candidate in St Mawes. The delight at winning was short-lived as it created a frisson of conflict in their household as Bill and Gregory found themselves on opposite sides over the introduction of regional planning systems. However they set-out to resolve any differences ensuring their personal life was able to continue in its same comfortable fashion and when the CPRE were victorious there was no animosity between them.

Gregory was heavily involved in the Arts and Culture scene. He and Bill were supporters of the Ballet Club, introduced by Arnold Haskell who was at Cambridge at the same time as Gregory. Arnold's mother, Emmy, was the champion for Alicia Markova who in 1925 danced as 'Nightingale' in Le Chant du Rassignoi's performance wearing Matisse's 'new-fangled' leotard.

Whilst at Trinity, mixing with Elton and Haskell, Gregory picked up a keen interest in the performing arts; it was something he continued to dabble in throughout his life. He became Chairman of the Cornwall Radio and Television

Company with a vision of bringing entertainment to the masses. However this venture never prospered sufficiently and Gregory was forced to voluntarily wind up the company. He appointed DC Ferry of Newquay as liquidator and a General Meeting of the Members was held on 3ʳᵈ October 1951 for Mr Ferry to pass an Extraordinary Resolution as to the disposal of books, accounts and documents.

Gregory's next financial venture was more successful, perhaps because of the advice his old friend, Elton, was able to impart. Both men are listed in the 1947 Kinematograph Year Book. Elton is listed twice, once within the 'Who's What in the Industry' when his short bio shows: ARTHUR ELTON, director, Film Centre Ltd.; b. 1906; educated Marlborough and Cambridge. Scenario department, Gainsborough 1927; E.M.B. Film Unit 1930; G.P.O. Film Unit 1934: producer to Minister. The second time was under 'Trade Organisations' and shows Elton as the President of The Scientific Film Association, based at Soho Square and Glasgow.

Gregory's entry was under 'The Leading Kinema Circuits'; he is shown as a Director of Cornwall Cinemas (Newquay) Ltd, based at Restormel, Mount Wise in Newquay. The business was originally set up by Geoffrey Taylor and there were five directors in total, including Gregory. They bought existing cinemas including the St Columb cinema, run initially by AE Hamblin. In addition they set up new ones, sometimes in unusual places; the cinema in Trevelyan, which opened in 1946, was in an old chapel bungalow.

During the war they toured the country with a mobile cinema showing films to the troops, continuing to grow the business where they could. By the 1960s they ended up running 12 cinemas in Cornwall.

In addition to these projects, Gregory became involved in the 'The Cornwall Club' and was Secretary when the club finally ceased in 1959. The club was created in 1792 and established as a public county library to 'illustrate the antiquities and natural history of Cornwall in all its branches'. It combined Gregory's love of literature and history, so it was a role he relished. The Club owned books, pamphlets, reviews, fossils and other artefacts; they also invited contributions from the local clergy and gentry of local information on agriculture, the weather and population. Access was by subscription and subscribers could either use the reading room or borrow the books.

In his final years Uncle Gregory lived at Richmond Hill, Truro, the house Bill and he had moved to when their original house was demolished as part of a road widening scheme. He died there on 18th December 1968, still the jovial giant so recognisable by everyone.

Pious Yudhishthira

Robert Arthur Godwin-Austen was born in 1864 out in Srinafar, Cashmere, India. His father was Lieutenant-Colonel Henry Haversham Godwin-Austen, the English topographer, geologist, naturalist and surveyor who surveyed the Himalayas and glaciers at the base of K2; it was not unusual to see the name of Mt Godwin-Austen on maps up until the 1950s.

His mother, Pauline, died after bearing two sons; her eldest son, Pious' brother, died at the age of 24 years. In later life Pious placed a brass plaque in the Shalford Parish Church in memory of his mother; although she had died when he was only five years old, his memories of her were all fond.

The family owned and resided at Shalford House until Henry ran into financial difficulties and was forced to sell off a number of family heirlooms. The situation could not be salvaged though and in 1898 Henry was declared bankrupt; he was forced to move out of Shalford House, letting it to a boys' school before it became used as a hotel in 1936. The remaining estate was put into trust and many of the buildings began to fall into disrepair, including the water mill which the Gang later saved.

For twenty five years Henry lived off his limited income, but his fortunes never recovered. Having been born into great wealth he died in 1924 with a mere £4,000 in today's value to his name.

The young Pious epitomised his father's life; he followed the family tradition of pursuing a military career, joining the British Army as his father had done. He studied at the Royal Military College, being promoted from cadet to Lieutenant in

1883. Shortly after that he was posted down to Plymouth as a Captain in the Dorset Regiment, the same one as Red Biddy's father, where he lived in lodgings with his fellow officers. He finally retired from His Majesty's Army in 1908, having risen to the rank of Major in 1893.

Upon retiring he returned to the family estate, taking up residency at Smithbrook Grange, Cranleigh with his elderly aunt Beatrice and one servant as company; a far cry from the grand Shalford House of his childhood.

It was at this time that the Gladstone family moved into the village and sharing a number of mutual friends and interests began to socialise with the Godwin-Austen family. Pious' father and John Gladstone, Bill's father, had an interest in antiquities; they were concerned with preserving their local history, something which Bill, Erb and Pious obviously inherited. Both fathers were members of the Surrey Archaeological Society.

Pious suffered the same damaging financial difficulties as his father, never being able to live within his limited income. The year after his father died, and with no large inheritance being forthcoming, he was declared bankrupt having to give up Smithbrook Grange, living somewhat nomadically with friends, perhaps trying to outwit people he owed money to. The petitioning creditors certainly had no knowledge of his residence or place of business at that time.

Things began to change a few years later though; in 1931, after 57 years of bachelordom, Pious married Kathleen Odling, a woman almost half his age. Kathleen was the daughter of a retired tea planter, living at Belsize Park, London, and her father may well have been someone the Godwin-Austens had known out in Cashmere.

The same year Bill and Agatha, meeting up with the newly married couple who were back living at Smithbrook Manor, saw the abandoned water mill at Shalford; with the recent SPAB campaign to save vernacular water mills fresh in their minds and with Bill eager for a project to start saving, they fortified the Gang into action and began a protracted, but effective, plan for Ferguson's Gang to raise the money to buy the water mill. Six months later the National Trust acquired the

157

property from the three trustees, Pious, Michael Forbes Tweedie and Ernest Horsford Bingham, the acting liquidator.

Four years later Pious, as trustee, also sold The Chantries to Guildford Borough Council so they could preserve and protect the southern aspect views of Guildford; two years after this the Council then bought Shalford House and Park for the same reason.

Having spent the last years of his life living off Kathleen's benefices, Pious died on 27th October 1948 leaving, like Bill, no worldly possessions.

Poolcat

George Macaulay Trevelyan was born on 16th February 1876 at the large house owned by his maternal grandfather in Welcombe, Warwickshire. His father, Sir George Otto Trevelyan the 2nd Baronet of Wallington, was a British Statesman who had twice been Secretary of State for Scotland under Prime Minister Gladstone. He was also a writer and historian, something which his son inherited. Poolcat's mother, Caroline, was the daughter of Robert Philips, MP for Bury. It is no wonder that these political antecedents spawned a continuation of the political clan; Poolcat's oldest brother, Sir Charles Trevelyan, a Liberal politician ended up joining the Labour party and served under Ramsay MacDonald.

Poolcat attended Harrow School before going up to Trinity College, Cambridge; here he became a member of the secret society – The Cambridge Apostles and is acclaimed as the founder of the 'Lake Hunt' a human hare and hounds chase.

There are great similarities between the Cambridge Apostles and Ferguson's Gang; both had updates from members at meetings; for the Apostles these were recorded in 'The Arc' and for the Gang it was in their 'Boo'; both demanded an oath of secrecy to be taken and the reading of a curse within the initiation ceremony. They also had members with strong Communist convictions; Guy Burgess and Kim Philby were Apostles and Red Biddy's political sympathies have been well documented.

Interestingly both groups forged strong lifelong bonds with the other members that went beyond the normal transient college friendships.

In 1904 Poolcat married Janet Penrose Ward and they went to live in Cheyne Gardens, Chelsea, becoming near neighbours of Red Biddy's family. They had three children here, Mary, Theodore and Charles, although devastatingly they lost Theo when he died from appendicitis aged just five. At the time they rented a weekend cottage in Surrey, near the village of Cranleigh which is where the Gladstones and the Trevelyans would meet up; John Gladstone and Poolcat both knowing each other through the Archaeological Society and their mutual friendship with Thomas Cecil and Williams-Ellis.

During the Great War Poolcat was declared unfit for military service due to defective eyesight; instead he became Commandant of the first British Red Cross ambulance unit to be sent to Italy. For three years Poolcat transported wounded soldiers from behind the trenches to hospital. This dedication to the charity may well have been an inspiration to Sister Agatha when she elected to become involved with the Red Cross during the Second World War.

Poolcat came from one of England's aristocratic families; the Trevelyans owned two estates; one in Cumbria and one in Warwickshire, together with a baronetcy through his paternal grandfather. Poolcat though was an unassuming quiet man, occasionally brusque but never rude. He would enjoy long walks of thirty or forty miles, just like Prime Minister Gladstone and CS Lewis.

It was this combination of inherited wealth, interest in history and enjoyment of England's fine open spaces that led him to become such a strong advocate of the National Trust. In 1924 he used his friendship with Stanley Baldwin, Lord Beershop's relation, and John Buchan, the author, to garner additional backing for the National Trust's cause. Poolcat became a member of the Council for the Trust in 1926, just a year before Ferguson's Gang was formed, and he stayed involved until the year before his death.

During the 1920s he was appointed Professor of Modern History at Trinity College, Cambridge where Uncle Gregory was one of his students. Having met Red Biddy as a child and inspired Bill during her teenage years, Poolcat went on to arouse Gregory's historical sentiments as a student. It was no wonder that he became an integral part of the Gang's supporters.

In 1929 Poolcat published his pamphlet *Must England's Beauty Perish?* helping, like the Gang's BBC appeal, to generate public interest. Throughout those interwar years he remained a passionate supporter of Ferguson's Gang, influencing the Executive wherever possible to help the complex negotiations required for the Gang to be able to purchase Shalford Mill, the Old Town Hall and Priory Cottages.

Poolcat stayed living in Cambridge for the rest of his life; he died the same year as Black Maria on 26th July 1962, leaving a hole in Bill's life.

The Birmingham Set: Joshua Bottle-Washer, Jerry Boham and Sam

Three of the other Gang members who were lifelong friends were Joshua Bottle-Washer, Jerry Boham and Sam. Jerry attended the AGM in 1934, reporting back on Hamer's retirement; Jerry and Joshua provided the 'letter patient' authorising Bill Stickers to open the new headquarters in place of Ferguson and Joshua wrote on behalf of Sam and Jerry to Bill when they sent down £6 3s in 'silver bullion' to use on the old cross (presumably the Whiteleaf Cross appeal) with the rest going to the Newtown project.

The paper used for this letter gave the greatest clue as to who these three were. It was a sample page produced by Kalamazoo Works in Northfield from the range of Kalamazoo Casebooks for Doctors, sent by George Oaks.

Kalamazoo was set up in 1913 by Oliver Moorland and Paul Impey, a Quaker who was friendly with the neighbouring Cadbury family, and who presumably also knew Silent O'Moyle. The business produced the famous loose leaf ledger which helped the company to grow and prosper. This Birmingham connection points to Lord Beershop and her three childhood friends, particularly when one of them was living in Birmingham at this time.

Joshua Bottle-Washer

Mabel Thomazine Mary Lyde was the daughter of William Henry Lyde, a silversmith who was a business associate of Is Nibs, Beershop's father. She was born in 1896 the youngest of six children; she grew up at Holly Bank, Kings Norton before moving to Forest Road in Moseley.

The family business started at Warstone Lane before moving to more prestigious premises on Constitution Hill and then finally to Newhall Hill where Joshua and her siblings lived when they weren't at the family home Boscobel House, Four Oaks, Sutton Coldfield, the same area as Fred.

Her father died in 1923 and soon afterwards the silver electroplate business was sold to George Unite and Sons. William left the family almost a million pounds in current values which meant that Joshua never had to work. Instead she spent her time on charitable works at home when she wasn't at her holiday house Heatherbank in Barmouth or travelling on one of her expeditions. These charitable works obviously included supporting Ferguson's Gang.

Joshua loved the thrill of exploring the world, in 1930 she took the Hildebrand liner to go on a cruise down the Amazon; two years later she headed off for a Mediterranean cruise aboard the Arandora Star; and in 1936 she travelled over to Vancouver on the Pacific Grove, along the Panama Canal and stopped at Los Angeles and San Francisco en-route.

Joshua never married, she stayed living with her mother after her father passed away, joining Beershop on the ambulance teams during the war and always returning to Sutton Coldfield after her adventures. She died there in 1970.

Jerry Boham

Margaret Wylie was born in 1914 to John and Lily Wylie. Her father moved down from Scotland to study law and lived with his aunt's family for over twenty years. During this time Lily Janet Walker, originally from Bromsgrove, also lodged with the family at Edge Hill Farm, Hill Hook, in Sutton Coldfield.

When the farm was sold and John's uncle retired, the family and their permanent lodgers moved to Hollyfield Road. By this time John was 49 and Lily was 29; the move may have prompted their betrothal; after knowing each other for almost half their lives they were finally married in 1913. A year later their only daughter was born.

John continued to practice as a barrister, earning respect for his professional reputation, culminating in the King, by Warrant under His Majesty's Royal Sign Manual, appointing John Wylie, Barrister-at-law to be Recorder of the Borough of Smethwick. He died in 1937 aged 72; Jerry was just 18 years old.

She continued to live at 203 Lichfield Road with her mother, just like Joshua, helping Sam with her nursery school and joining the ambulance service along with the others. When Lily died on 1st February 1964 she left Jerry with a fortune worth almost half a million pounds by today's values.

Sam

Mary Louise Perkins was born on 25th September 1907. The Perkins family lived on Victoria Road, Sutton Coldfield and her father was Arthur Watson Perkins, a draper whose shop was on Mill Street, a traditional concern that closed early on a Thursday afternoon, as was the practice in the town at the time. Sam had an older brother, Samuel Watson Perkins, a family name that had been passed down through the generations, so it was only natural that she took 'Sam' as her pseudonym.

Coming from a working middle-class family it was expected that Sam would earn her own money. Before the Second World she ran a children's nursery school, helped by Jerry Boham.

Sam, like the other two, never married and continued to live at the family home on Lichfield Road. She worked on the ambulances throughout the war, however she died soon after the war had finished, having suffered complications during a nasal operation. She died aged 41.

Sister Niphite

Isabelle Henrietta Granger was the older sister of Sister Agatha; the name is a play both on their relationship and on Agatha's pseudonym. Niphite was born on 20th January 1906 at Hill House, Maldon. Like Agatha, Niphite attended the Maldon Grammar School before boarding at Saint Felix School and becoming friends with Shoubersky.

A natural academic, Niphite went up to Newnham College, Cambridge in 1924 taking her degree in modern languages. While she was there she met Bill Stickers, and through this connection, Bill and Agatha first met.

After graduating from Newnham, Niphite went to teach at Channing School in Highgate; the school was founded in 1885 for the education of daughters of Unitarian Ministers. When Niphite joined the teaching staff there were 125 girls attending, six of whom had assistance from private benefactions. The school grounds were both extensive and beautiful, having originally been part of Sir Sydney Waterlow's park and it contained an ancient cedar tree that was planted in the 1800s. During this time Niphite lived at Fairseat, Highgate Hill in a shared house with other women from the school.

While working here she took some time out one summer to sail over to New York on one of the Cunard liners for a break. Niphite remained teaching at the school until the outbreak of war, still studying for her Master's Degree which she finally achieved in 1942. However a stray parachute mine badly damaged the school and Niphite was forced to move away. She turned from teaching to taking a variety of secretarial and assistant jobs, whilst living at Haverstock Hill. She worked as a clerk at the National Assistance Board, the start of the Welfare State; an archivist at Farrer & Co, the legal firm whose clients included the British Royal family; within Town and Country Planning and for the Ministry of Information on Overseas Publications. It was through this work that she was awarded silver medals for her services to the Austrian and Italian Governments.

While Sister Agatha passionately championed the English countryside and heritage, Sister Niphite was an impassioned social reformer. After the war she became far more active in working towards social change, not caring what society thought. As well as being a single mother (she adopted a daughter), she wrote papers on adoption and illegitimacy, something she felt very strongly about. She was General Secretary for the National Council for Unmarried Mother & her Child for almost twenty years; returning to teaching as a Department Tutor for the ILEA Homes and Hospital and finally working as Organisation Secretary for the Union Girls' School for Social Service. During this time she moved to Gayton Crescent, Swiss Cottage, presumably to create a home with her daughter.

Throughout her life she was involved in charity works, over and above those she participated in with the Gang. She was a voluntary worker with refugees before the war and a regular prison visitor at Holloway after the war. She was also a ward visitor at Charing Cross for cancer sufferers. Ever the sociable butterfly, Niphite continued to throw parties for the Gang members and their supporters well into later life. She died the same year as Lord Beershop in 1990.

Lord Beershop's Advisors

In addition to the fourteen conscripted members who are named here, there are a further two who are spoken about in the Boo. These are the Lord Beershop's Advisors (or 'Is Advisors as they are refered to), namely Wilfred and Bertha Sherwood. Their pseudonyms are Is Nibs (which refers to Beershop's father) and Outer Yam Yam which refers to her mother. Yam yam is a Black Country term which Birmingham residents use when referring to people from the neighbouring area (including Sutton Coldfield). This once again shows Bill's witty humour in using local idioms when creating the pseudonyms.

Mother Maudez

The name is one of Bill Stickers' witty inventions; Saint Maudez is a Breton saint from the 600s. The name has a number of derivatives includes Saint Mawes in Cornwall. Although it was not clear who Mother Maudez is, there is a clear pointer that the name was from one of Bill's Cornwall friends who was living near Truro at the time. The most likely candidate is the Rev.

Hunkin; someone who supported her fully in her philanthropic endeavours. The term 'mother' being a play on his clerical 'Father' title (Mother Maudez translating into Father of Mawes).

Chapter Eleven: Cause Célèbre Members

There are a number of other supporters including Forward Amanda and Old Poll of Paddington. We know Anne of Lothbury was a benefactor to the National Trust in her own right but there is no clear indication of her true identity. There are two others who were intimately involved with the Gang although their actual noms-de-guerre are unknown; these two people are AP Herbert and CS Lewis.

AP Herbert

Sir Alan Patrick Herbert was a novelist, playwright and law reform activist. He was linked to Ferguson's Gang through a number of mutual friends. He was an independent Member of Parliament for Oxford University from 1935 to 1950, at the time CS Lewis was a lecturer there. He also worked with John Ferguson in the 1920s on a series of one act plays, giving Bill an introduction through her mentor.

In 1940 Herbert visited the Gang's headquarters, sharing their love of The Thames summed up in their private song:

'The Westbourne, Tyburn, Walbrook, Fleet,
We swears it on their grave,
There shall no treasures more be lost
That Ferguson's Gang can save.'

They persuaded Herbert to take part in the 'oly X.Cursion to collect 'oly Fleet water and from the London Thames. The proceedings are recorded in the second Boo.
'Silent and Is B. quickly hid on board the State Barge while Bill collected Kate, the Artichoke and Shot Biddy. APH then propelled the State Barge 2 the mouth of the Fleet; and the Beershop choosing Kate as Is Aconite. They and the Artichoke were cast loose in a samfan, which the Artichoke rowed valiantly against the strong current towards a sinister double tunnel intersected by a black Coffin. Up the right hand tunnel the samfan disappeared, according 2 Is B impelled or sucked by

166

unseen 4cc. Their return was anxiously awaited, in view of the raucous yells of ghouls in the adjoining seminary. They emerged at last triumphantly bearing a bottle of Oly Fleet Water.

'APH then made the Wallbrook which came sprouting 4th in white waves under Cannon Street Bridge. Bill and Biddy were rowed by the Artichoke in the teeth of a pleece current, and wading ashore they walked up a dangerous Beach deep in sharp edged foreign bodies 2 the spouting Wallbrook, at which they filled a bottle. On their return they eard the pheares baying of the Dog Cerebos, but lived above it.

'APH then moored the State Barge alongside the one of a minor River Deity whose Den was inspected, and then attaching the Barge 2 a Rochester Spitty Barge we sang Oly Songs 2 Bill's goitre and had a nice meal the Beershop having presented a bottle of the Gang's Sloe Gin 2 APH, he kindly drunk our elth in a loving mug, and so did we all. Then he propelled the State Barge under Tower Bridge which burst 4 us 2 pass through and as the full moon rose like a bad orange, we returned very appy and grateful 2 Hungerford Steps. An un4gettable outing 2 be classed with Stonehenge and Newtown and the National Trust Banquet as one of the Gang's Great Pleasures.'

The samples of the tributary waters, so carefully collected, can still be seen at Shalford Mill today.

CS Lewis

Clive Staples Lewis, like Herbert, had a number of connections with Bill Stickers and Ferguson's Gang. On 19th September 1914, Lewis went to study at Great Bookham, Surrey with WT Kirkpatrick 'The Great Knock'. He remained here, within the Gladstone's neighbourhood, for three years in preparation for going up to Oxford. Kirkpatrick had been Lewis' father's Head Master at Lurgan College and he had already successfully helped prepare Lewis' brother, Warnie, for admission to the Royal Military College at Sandhurst. Bill, therefore, knew of the young Lewis while she was growing up.

The relationship was strengthened after both had left university through the mutual friendship with Alfred Jenkin. He and Lewis had been friends at Oxford where both were members of the Martlets Literary Society; Jenkin and Bill were both Cornish Bards.

Lewis and Herbert, as contemporaries, worked together as contributors to the published work 'Time and Tide' which came out in 1954 and must have spoken of their friends within the Gang.

Lewis, like Bill and Poolcat, was concerned with the loss of open countryside to over-development. 'This place is being ruined by buildings... where will it end? If we live to be old there will hardly be any real country left in the south of England' he wrote to his brother.

Lewis may well have influenced the Gang on two of their appeals; Whiteleaf Cross and The Priory Cottages. In his letter, again to his brother, in 1932 he had written about his friend Foord-Kelsie taking him over to visit the village of Kimble in the Chilterns, where Foord-Kelsie had previously been the Rector. 'Whenever we passed a rash of bungalows or a clutch of petrol pumps, he was at his usual game. 'How ridiculous to pretend that these things spoiled the beauty of the countryside etc.' Late in the day, and now in his own country [Kimble], he waved his hand towards a fine hillside and remarked 'My old friend Lee – a most remarkable man – bought all that and presented it to the nation to save it from being covered with bungalows'.' Lewis loved the irony of his friend's view and encouraged the Gang to help save the rest of the Whiteleaf Cross site.

Lewis' conversion to Christianity whilst travelling to Whipsnade in a side car in 1931 is well-documented; it was a revelation similar to Bill's conversion to Catholicism. He began to take an interest in local theology and the rich vein of religious history around Oxford. On his regular long walks from The Kilns, Headington, he would often pass through the villages of Abingdon and Steventon. He wrote to his brother 'You and I have hitherto entirely underrated Abingdon. Their [sic] is a church standing in a quadrangle of alms-houses right down on one of these little fresh water wharves on the river...' This was similar to The Priory Cottages at Steventon that he also saw, a group of timber monastic buildings that once belonged to the Priory at Steventon. One of Lewis' fellows from Oxford, CRJ

168

Currie included it within his work on smaller domestic architecture. The property also featured in *A history of the county of Berkshire* published in 1924. Lewis called upon the Gang to save the Priory Cottages when the family put it up for sale after the death of Mrs Langford.

Lewis and Bill kept up a lengthy correspondence throughout their lives; both were avid letter writers and keen to share experiences of day to day life. The friendship culminated in Bill's embroidery of Lewis' Chronicles of Narnia tales which was undertaken as a tribute to her dear friend.

Chapter Twelve: Newest Recruits

Although Ferguson's Gang is no longer the pioneering force it was during the interwar years, the Gang still continues to attract support for its cause.

Joyce Conwy-Evans

In 1989 Sister Agatha took one last pilgrimage to the Town Hall, a site which held so many happy memories for her of the Gang. She abandoned her mask and disguise for the day and presented a collage designed and decorated by Joyce Conwy-Evans. The two of them handed over the collage, which related to the Old Town Hall on the Isle of Wight, to the National Trust.

Joyce, like the Gang, is a somewhat enigmatic figure. She met Sister Agatha in the 1960s at Glyndebourne and became a firm friend of both Sister Agatha's and the rest of the Gang. She recalled Sister Niphite organising parties at her house for the Gang, events which were always overflowing with bonhomie and jests. She also stayed with Sister Agatha for weekends down at Cawdles Barn and although she was a friend of the Gang, it appears Joyce was never bestowed with a pseudonym, simply retaining her own name.

Joyce studied at Bromley College before going to the Royal College of Art and setting up her own embroidery and design practice in 1974. Her work includes a 20' tapestry for the Hilton Hotel on Park Lane, 'The Elements' for Eastbourne Water Works and robe edgings and trumpet tabard for her old Alma Mater the Royal College of Art. In 1981, like Beershop, Joyce designed several altar frontals including King's College Chapel, Cambridge and the Chapel of Martyrs and Saints in Canterbury Cathedral.

Sister Agatha invited Joyce and Geoffrey Parsons to go with her to hand over the Gang's room to the National Trust and to fix the glass case to the wall. This contained the Gang's treasured collection of bottles of Thames tributary water. There was a celebration tea in the meadow to mark the auspicious occasion.

Twenty years later Joyce was commissioned by Sister Agatha to design the collage relating to the Old Town Hall which would be presented to the National Trust. There were careful instructions on which of the Gang's names should appear, the illustrations to be used and references inferred. The octopus of course is shown in glory, as too is a mouse. However the reason for including this humble creature is lost in the mists of time and searching through the Gang's records has not yielded any answer.

Joyce accompanied Agatha, still as a Ferguson Gang member, to present her finished collage in 1989. As they handed it over Sister Agatha reminded everyone why the Gang had been so dedicated to the Trust's cause: 'We cared about helping to save England and wanted to be involved in something of permanent value.' The presentation of the collage was a reminder of the essential part the Gang played in preserving some of the National Trust's sites.

Dutch Doll

In 1994 Sarah Jane Forder, the Editor of the National Trust's Magazine contacted Bill Stickers regarding the centenary celebrations of the Trust and enquired about the possibility of one last poem (similar to the ones she had created all those years ago as a young woman). Bill christened Forder 'The Dutch Doll' after a member of an all-women Arctic exploration team. Bill duly provided the poem which now forms part of the Trust's archives:

> For 100 years the Trust has fought
> And the Battle is still to win –
> You sit there moaning and wringing your hands?
> You say it's a shame and a sin?
>
> Hedges and fields and forests
> Vanishing one by one
> Get your pen and your cheque book out –
> Load to fire your gun!
> Save what is left of England,
> Give what you can and more –

Once in the hands of the National Trust
It is safe for evermore
And thanks to the sacrifice you make,
The wild flowers will increase,
The bird and the beast and the butterfly
Shall breed and thrive in peace.'

Dutch Doll also invited Bill to the celebrations but in true Gang style Bill politely declined declaring: 'I ave always preferred 2 be euonymus and I done wot I could while I could'.

Pegasus

Judging from the discoveries, the last official recruit to Ferguson's Gang was conscripted in 1996. On Bill Sticker's death she wrote to The Times, requesting that they run one final appeal for Ladye Park; to this end she appointed Pegasus as the Gang's representative, entrusting a copy of this letter to Michael Maine.

Pegasus had known Bill Stickers from his childhood; he had grown up in Cornwall and a shared love of organ music forged a friendship that spanned their disparate years. He had been a choral scholar in the choir of the Truro Cathedral as a child and went on to study the organ with John Winter, the Organist and Master of the Choristers.

His recollections of Bill's reminiscences formed part of the museum's collection at the Old Town Hall, giving a fascinating portrayal of Bill's earlier life.

Bill Sticker's influence on Pegasus penetrated his life, as well as taking up the mantle as the final Gang member, he underwent a similar religious conversion resulting in him pursuing ordination.

172

Chapter Thirteen: Final Word

All of the original inner circle members of Ferguson's Gang have passed away; so too have most of their loyal supporters and subscribers. The National Trust is no longer a fledging society with only a handful of members; it has grown from a few thousand into being the second largest organisation in the UK.

The world that Ferguson's Gang knew has long since disappeared; a world of genteel tea-parties, grand country houses and armies of servants; where women were expected to be social hostesses and to confine their outlook to their home, husband and children.

We are no longer seeing the tragic loss of so many of our great aristocratic houses, women are not forced to fight for suffrage and acceptance; nor do we face the same class challenges of earlier generations. Through the National Trust and other similar charitable bodies, many of our historically important homes and landscapes are being preserved and cared for better than at any time before. Many of these are open to all, ensuring their viability and accessibility for future generations.

But for all that the fight continues. The old guard of Ferguson's Gang may now have retreated after a lifetime's dedication to the cause but their mission and zeal is still needed today. The work to preserve our truly unique Englishness, with its vernacular architecture and regional flavour, needs to go on. In the last words of Bill Stickers '...his final request is that the gang be opened to all...' There will always be the necessity for a guardian of our history to conserve our gems and jewels and to do so sympathetically so that they continue to be used and appreciated.

Almost a century after Bill Stickers devised the idea of an anonymous group of disguised bandits and formed Ferguson's Gang with four of her dearest friends, the mystery has been solved. Those mysterious maidens behind the masks have finally been revealed. In doing so, it is hoped that the unveiling pays the due reverence to their daring antics and spirited approach to life which they deserve.

The journey of discovery to track down the Ferguson's Gang members was never straight-forward for they covered their tracks well. Although twenty six of the Gang have had their true identities revealed here, there still remain a number of supporters lurking within the shadows, waiting for recognition of their hard and unstinting assistance to the Gang. Pore Old Harris, Samson, Anne of Lothbury, Sister Boadicea, Old Poll of Paddington, Matheson, Dulce, Forward Amanda and Volker Jake have yet to be revealed.

Just as the fight for the cause to preserve our English architectural heritage needs to continue, so perhaps too does this journey of discovery. It appears that Ferguson's Gang still manages to retain some of their intriguing mystery.

Sources of Reference:

A Century for Cornwall. Brown, H. Miles. Blackford (1976)

A History of the County of Middlesex: Volume 6: Friern Barnet, Finchley, Hornsey with Highgate (1980)

A Noble thing – The national trust and its benefactors, Merlin Waterson. Scala Publishers Ltd

America's First Frogman: The Draper Kauffman Story, Elizabeth Kauffman Bush. Naval Institute Press (15 June 2012)

Amphitheatre project, Chester.gov.uk

Architect and Building News (12 June 1942)

Architect Errant, Williams-Ellis, Clough. Constable 0216910234

Artists Rifles: Regimental Roll of Honour and War Record 1914–1919 (3rd ed.), Higham, S Stagoll (2006) [1922, Howlett & Son]. Naval & Military Press 9781847341297

Austen, Henry Haversham Godwin- (1834–1923), Oxford Dictionary of National Biography. Oxford University Press

Avebury. The National Trust (2009)

Bergman Österberg Union Archive, North West Kent College

Bert Firman, Wright, John

Bristol University Archives

Cambridge University

Communist Party Magazine, Focus

Cornwall Records office

Cornwall, Peggy Pollard. Paul Elek Publishers

Country houses: the lost legacy, Worsley, Giles. The Telegraph (15 June 2002)

Council for the Protection of Rural England Archives

Daily Mail (3 October 1934)

Diana Jervis-Read

Dictionary of Scottish Architects: William Weir

Discovering Tong, Its History, Myths and Curiosities, Jeffery, Robert. Privately Published (2007) 0955508908

Edinburgh Gazette (17 April 1908)

England and the Octopus, Trustees of Clough Williams-Ellis

England's lost Houses, Worsley, Giles. Aurum Press (2002) 1854108204

Essex Record Office

Evening News (2 February 1933)

Evening News (1932)

Feonix Paranormal Ltd (2011)

Ferguson, Bagnall Polly (2012)

Folkestone Gazette

Folkestone Library

Fortnum & Mason

Geoff Taylor Educational Trust

Girton College

Glasgow Herald

Glimpses of the College, Bowers, Mary

Grand Hotels, Denby, Elaine

Haggard, Lilias Margitson Rider, Who Was Who. A & C Black

Hansard (14 December 1933) vol 284 c530

Harrods

Henry Head: The Man and His Ideas, Brain R (1961)

History Centre Surrey

Inside Outsider: The Life and Times of Colin MacInnes, Tony Gould. Penguin
        (1983)

Ironbridge Museum

Isle of Wight County Press Online (3 March 1934)

Joyce Conwy-Evans

Just the weather for a seaside trip. The Times Beaulieu (02 November 1996)

Kensington Central library

Kinematograph Year Book (1947)

King's College archives

Listing info SJ4812SE ST JOHN'S HILL

London Gazette (14 December 1945)

London Gazette (17 July 1951)

London Gazette (1945)

London Gazette (2 May 1924)

London Gazette (7 January 1936)

London Gazette (9 March 1883)

Mark Matlach

Meacham: A Historical Tour around Erdington 1986-1987

Metropole Advertisement

Metropole Building. Ministry of Defence

Must England's Beauty Perish, GM Trevelyan. Faber & Gwyer Limited (1929)

National Trust (March 1938)

National Trust 1934 Annual Report

National Trust 1935 Annual Report

National Trust 1936 Annual Report

National Trust 1938 Annual Report

National Trust Acquisitions Up to December 2011, An historical summary of
        Trust acquisitions (including covenants)

National Trust Exhibition

National Trust Magazine, Sue Herdman (2008)

National Trust News (February 1936)

National Trust website

Newnham College Register

Newquay Voice (30 January 2004)

Obituary Notices of Fellows of the Royal Society, Holmes, G. (1941)

Obituary: Lieut.-Colonel Henry Haversham Godwin-Austen

Old Felicians Association

Oxford Dictionary of National Biography, Brooke, Justin. Oxford University
        Press (2004)
Oxford National Dictionary of Biography, Murdoch, Brian. Oxford University
        Press
Papers of Dr Rachel Pinney. Archives Hub. University of Manchester
Parishes: Steventon', A History of the County of Berkshire: Volume 4 (1924)
Penguin Books Archives
Philosophy in the modern world - Google Books
Pinney, Maj.-Gen. Sir Reginald (John) Who Was Who (Online ed.). A & C
        Black (2007)
Playing the Game: Sport and the Physical Emancipation of English Women,
        McCrone, Kathleen E. Routledge (1988) 041500358X
Prehistoric Britain from the air: a study of space, time and society, Darvill,
        Timothy. Cambridge University Press (1996) 9780521551328
Railway Times, Kew Archives
Red Cross Museum and Archive
Richard Ford Manuscripts
Royal Academy of Music Magazine, In memoriam. Royal Academy of Music
        Library (1945)
Ruskin's Fors Clavigera Letter V (1871) from England and the Octopus
Sandplay past present and future, Mitchell, Rie Rogers, Friedman, Harriet S
Scottish Episcopal Clergy, 1689-2000, Bertie, David M
Sir George Otto, Bart Trevelyan Encyclopædia Britannica, Volume 27
Slade School of Art Archives
Stamford Brook: an affectionate portrait, Reginald Coleman Shirley Seaton.
        Stamford Brook Publications 0951889613
St Elphin's Magazine (1925)
Surrey Heritage Centre
The Adelaide Chronicle (16 April 1927)
The Annual Journal Of The Downhill Only Club (7 February 1952)
The Arts and Crafts Movement: a study of its sources, ideals and influence on
        design theory, Naylor, Gillian. Studio Vista (1971) 028979580X
The Barrier Miner (5 January 1940)
The Boo
The Builder (24 April 1936)
The Carefree Smuggler, GFG Pollard. Grant Richards
The Children's Newspaper (2 December 1933)
THE COLLECTED LETTERS OF CS LEWIS VOL II by CS Lewis ©
        copyright CS Lewis Pte Ltd 2004
The Daily Express (November 1933)
The Daily Sketch (Tuesday 7 November 1933)
The day a Russian prince in an England shirt beat the All Blacks, Gallagher,
        Brendan. The Telegraph (2006)
The Edinburgh Gazette (17 July 1925)
The Guardian (8 November 1995)

The Gender Agenda. The Independent (2 July 2003)

The Glasgow Herald (1909)

The Glasgow Herald (9 Sept 1970)

The Illustrators: the British art of illustration, 1800–2007 Nickerson, Fiona; Wootton, David. Chris Beetles (2007) 1905738056

The Independent (12 July 1996)

The Independent (1996)

The Independent (24 February 2013)

The Independent (7 August 1998)

The Morning Post (19 December 1934)

The Morning Post The Sunday Pictorial

The National Trust – the first hundred years, Waterson, Merlin. BBC Books (1994)

The People (23 December 1934)

The Second Boo National Trust

The Story of St Elphin's School 1844-1944, Flood, Margaret L

The Telegraph (11 December 2009)

The Telegraph (3 December 2004)

The Thirties – An intimate history, Juliet Gardiner. HarperPress (2011)

The Times (19 December 1934)

The Telegraph (19 December 1934)

The Times (1938)

The Times (7 November 1933)

The Morning Post (8 November 1933)

The Victoria Advertisement. www.historyworld.co.uk

The War the Infantry Knew 1914–1919: A Chronicle of Service in France and Belgium, Dunn, Captain J. C. Abacus (1994) 0349106355

Tonks, Henry The Oxford Dictionary of Art, Editor Ian Chilvers. Oxford University Press (2004)

Trevelyan, George Macaulay Alumni Cantabrigiense, Venn, J (online ed.). Cambridge University Press

The Last Whig Historian and Consensus History: George Macaulay Trevelyan, 1876–1962, Hernon, Jr. The American Historical Review (1976)

The Man in the Dark, Ferguson J (1952) Penguin Books

Virginia Woolf, Lee, Hermione (1996)

Volume 2 Newnham College Register (1924-1950)

Wellcome Library Archive

Women in the War Zone, Powell, Anne. The History Press 9780750950596

Women's Library

www.swmaritime.org.uk

www.unithistories.com

If you enjoyed this book why not take a look at the other titles available by the same author.

Available on Amazon or at any good bookshop.

Shop Talk

Life never turns out as you want…

Josie Carrington is a married carefree, shopaholic. Her life revolves around enjoying herself, thinking about having a baby and lunching with friends. Until her husband dies tragically.

Suddenly Josie finds that life as a penniless widow is no fun, but with her usual resolve she throws herself into trying to find a job although office work has never been her forte.

A bit of ingenuity, several good friends and a lucky break help Josie rediscover hidden talents, allowing her to forge ahead with a new life and deal with her mother's constant match-making.

Then, just as life seems to start to get back to normal, Josie faces the ultimate decision. Whatever she decides it can only mean more sadness.

At times like this sometimes only a good shop will do…

http://draytonbeauchampseries.moonfruit.com

Rural Affairs

Alicia's a smart sassy lawyer who won't stand for any nonsense. She lives for payday, Prada and becoming a Partner of the firm. Having shaken the proverbial rural dust of Drayton Beauchamp off her Jimmy Choos, she knows exactly what she wants out of life.

At least, until one disastrous summer, she thinks she does. Then, stuck back in the village she grew up in things start to get complicated as she rediscovers old friends, Matty the farmer's wife with a passion for fashion and Chloe, the eternal romantic. As she clashes with her mother's favourite gardener, deals with aggressive clients and sees her friend's marriage fall apart, she finds that she becomes inexplicably bound to the village. However much she tries to leave it appears fate has other plans.

Whoever said life in the countryside was boring couldn't have been more wrong; there's always a rural affair.

http://draytonbeauchampseries.moonfruit.com

Puppy Love Tales

Life is never dull in Drayton Beauchamp; but for Zoe it feels as though her world has been turned upside down.

As her elderly employer is rushed off to hospital and the dog rescue centre is set to close, she doesn't think it can get much worse…

Until a city developer and his girlfriend turn up and threaten to build a new housing estate on the beloved allotments.

With the village up in arms and the tensions rising, Zoe finds herself plunged into the centre of the controversy, with some dramatic unforeseen consequences. Everything falls apart, but luckily it turns out a dog really is a girl's best friend.

http://draytonbeauchampseries.moonfruit.com

Supporting the National Trust

While working on this book it became apparent that the on-going support for the National Trust is as vital today as it was in the 1930s.

Why not become one of Ferguson's Gang and pledge your support to the National Trust.

If you would like to make a difference then go to:

www.fergusonsgang.co.uk
or
https://join.nationaltrust.org.uk/donate/oneoff/

13481321R00115

Printed in Great Britain
by Amazon.co.uk, Ltd.,
Marston Gate.